PRAISE FOR *PRINCIPL..*

'I learnt a lot from Paul Browning's book – an in-depth study on what characterises good leadership. *Principled* is timely – well worth a read by all who are seeking to lead, particularly in the shadow of past wrongs and the legacy of leaders who have failed to understand what leadership requires.' — **Tim Costello AO, Chief Executive of World Vision Australia**

'*Principled* is a must-read book for all leaders. Every leader needs to earn trust and also understand that it can be lost in a moment. In a world where trust is in rapid decline, this book provides invaluable practical advice with useful case studies for leaders, on how to build and retain the precious commodity that is the trust of their followers and stakeholders.' — **Dr Kirstin Ferguson, Company Director and author of *Women Kind***

'If you have ever doubted the significance of a high trust culture read *Principled*. If you have ever underestimated the importance of a trustworthy leader read *Principled*. This book is a compelling, confronting, totally convincing account of why "Trusted Leadership" is at the heart of individual, collective and organisational wellbeing. But more, *Principled* provides what is needed most – the leadership practices to become more trustworthy.' — **Anthony Mackay AM, CEO National Center on Education & the Economy Washington DC**

'Trust is not blind faith, but underpins a rigour of shared values, and a preparedness to take measured risks, which is what drives performance. In *Principled*, Dr Browning presents a timely and important piece of work; of particular interest and relevance is the honest representation of the challenges leading an institution at the centre of a Royal Commission. In this situation, the critical role of building trust as a foundational underpinning of leading cultural change is well illuminated. *Principled* promotes a reflection on our own leadership, and where and how we might become more trusted and thus more effective leaders.' — **Lance Hockridge, former Managing Director of Aurizon and leader in the field of diversity**

'In *Principled*, Dr Paul Browning restores our faith in trust: what it looks like, how to gain it, what happens when we lose it. With practical wisdom learned from his own lived experiences, Dr Browning paints for us the portrait of a trustworthy, compassionate, principled leader – a model to which we can all aspire.' — **Leanne Kemp, Everledger Founder and Queensland's Chief Entrepreneur**

'Dr Paul Browning is one of Australia's truly distinguished educational leaders. *Principled* draws upon his deeply personal response to former students who were victims of abuse to provide exceptional foundational advice on ethical leadership behaviour and attitudes for educational and other institutional leaders.' — **Dr Roderick Kefford AM**

Dr Paul Browning has been a school principal for more than 20 years. He is currently Headmaster of St Paul's School in Brisbane, which has been listed among the world's 100 most innovative learning organisations in Cambridge University's Innovation 800 series, and Australian School of the Year for 2019. Paul is a sought-after guest-speaker in Australia and internationally, drawing from his evidence-based research *Compelling Leadership: The importance of trust and how to get it*. As reported in *The Courier-Mail*, Browning is 'one of the most respected and influential figures in education in the country'. He was awarded best non-government school principal in 2018 and is the recipient of the Miller-Grassie Award for Outstanding Leadership in Education for his contribution to research, literature and leadership.

Principled

10 leadership practices
for building trust

PAUL BROWNING

First published 2020 by University of Queensland Press

PO Box 6042, St Lucia, Queensland 4067 Australia

uqp.com.au
uqp@uqp.uq.edu.au

Cover design by Christabella Designs
Cover photograph by Shutterstock
Typeset in 12/16 pt Bembo Std by Post Pre-press Group, Brisbane
Printed in Australia by McPherson's Printing Group

A catalogue record for this book is available from the National Library of Australia

ISBN 978 0 7022 6271 5 (pbk)
ISBN 978 0 7022 6385 9 (pdf)
ISBN 978 0 7022 6386 6 (epub)
ISBN 978 0 7022 6387 3 (kindle)

'Leadership is an example of the life lived for others, because, as any truly effective leader knows, leadership is the ultimate form of service to a community, organisation or society.'

— Hugh Mackay, *The Good Life*

To the men and women who should have been kept safe by the institutions entrusted to their care when they were children. The crimes committed against them should never have been allowed to occur. This work serves as a reminder that failings of the past should never happen again: leadership should never be about the person, but rather, the people he or she serves.

CONTENTS

PREFACE

What is the single most important attribute a leader should have? Hundreds of thousands of people from all organisational spheres – corporate, not-for-profit and voluntary – have responded to that question, providing words that describe the leader they would most choose to follow. Consistently, decade after decade, the top word has been *trust*. We all long for leaders we can trust.

There is a well-worn trail of books and articles about trust and leadership, each offering their own perspective and wisdom on how to improve it. The *Harvard Business Review* regularly runs articles about trust. Robert Hurley, faculty member in the High Impact Leadership program for executives at Columbia Business School, surveyed 450 executives of 30 companies around the world. In his 2006 article, 'The Decision to Trust', he wrote, 'Roughly half of all managers don't trust their leaders', a sentiment that reinforced a growing trend.

A survey of Americans in 2002 found that a bleak 69 per cent of respondents agreed with the statement, 'I just don't know whom I can trust anymore.' Those figures were no better in 2015; in fact, they were possibly worse, with Statista, a statistics portal drawing upon 22,500 sources, stating that '80 per cent of people surveyed in 27 markets across the globe distrust their governments, businesses, or both, according to Edelman's Trust Barometer.'

For the past 20 years I have been the principal of two large non-government schools, with annual turnovers between $A20 and $40 million. My role as headmaster is not unlike that of a CEO of a not-for-profit organisation. I am responsible to a Board for all aspects of strategy, finance, risk, compliance, human resources, capital infrastructure, wellbeing and academic programs. While these two schools were from the non-government sector, they couldn't have been more different in terms of what was required from me in the leadership role.

My first appointment was as the founding head of a school that was going to be built in a new satellite city in the Australian Capital Territory (ACT). With the support of an excellent governing body and staff I was able to create an institution that was reflective of what I believed and valued about education: a place with a strong sense of community where relationships were central; educational programs that were inclusive and respected the strengths and gifts of each individual; and a strong connection and partnership with the school's owners, the Anglican Church. After ten years and two contract cycles, and having achieved the vision, I handed the reins to another principal to lead it through the consolidation phase.

My second appointment was equally challenging, but for completely different reasons. St Paul's School in Brisbane's north was about to celebrate its 50th anniversary and I was keen to further my leadership skills by moving to an established organisation. What I didn't realise in commencing this new role, what I totally underestimated, was the power of the prevailing culture. The culture had been shaped by historical events that had occurred at the school in the 1980s and 1990s, when more than 120 boys had been abused over the course of 17 years. The leadership style of the three previous heads in dealing with these issues, a style that contrasted starkly with my own, had a significant impact on the organisation. The year prior to my appointment, staff turnover was 30 per cent. The policies, systems and procedures created in response to the massive failings on the part of the school and its owners (the church) to keep students safe in the two decades before the turn of the century had the unintended consequence of all but extinguishing any hint of trust within the organisation.

I spent the first few months in my new role as principal, listening to each of the 220 staff. The overriding sense I gained from these conversations was a question framed in no uncertain terms: 'Browning, are you trustworthy?' Those who remained were either lucky enough not to have fallen victim to the 'toxic culture' that had been inadvertently created or had positioned themselves as 'heads-down' employees who obeyed instructions no matter how obscure or unreasonable. Many had taken extended leave to review their options. It was clear that staff were wounded by the practices that had become embedded as cultural norms, the unwritten rules and expectations that shaped the way staff worked and interacted with each other and the student body. One of those unwritten norms was that 'no-one is trustworthy until proven otherwise'. There was very little sense of teamwork or collaboration. Information was rarely shared; instead it was kept guarded so it could be used against others. Individuals were protective of their 'patch' and would seldom offer to help their co-workers. The practice of teaching occurred behind closed doors; colleagues were never invited into other classrooms to offer support, or provide feedback and mentoring. Following each lesson, teachers would scurry back to their desks avoiding any interaction with students that weren't necessary.

Then in 2013, five years after I started, the Royal Commission into Institutional Responses to Child Sexual Abuse was announced. The royal commission would go on to hold 57 formal public hearings, with St Paul's becoming the subject of one of those hearings. Over the course of two years, 100,000 pages of evidence from the school were collated and provided to the Commission, highlighting the untold damage that individuals, families and the broader school community had endured as a result of the abuse that occurred at the school.

It was during this time I first became aware of a former student, Archie, who had been blogging about his own story of abuse at the hands of former staff. For over 30 years, Archie had been carrying his burden in silence. After he learnt that his old school was to become a case study in the public hearing he started sharing a raw account of how he had suffered at the hands of two monsters: a senior student and a teacher. He was just thirteen. Not long after he went public with his accusations one of the perpetrators committed suicide, which quickly got picked up by the mainstream media and became front-page news.

As the principal, the school community turned to me to provide guidance, strength and leadership through what was a 'critical incident', albeit a very protracted one. Years earlier the community had endured a very public inquiry that ended in 2003 with the resignation of the then Governor-General of Australia, Dr Peter Hollingworth, for his mishandling of abuse in Anglican Schools in the Brisbane diocese when he was Archbishop. When the inquiry had concluded the school thought it could move on, putting the ugly story behind it. The history and pain was pushed below the surface, covered over with new cultural norms and a thin veneer of false hope. No-one wanted to revisit the past. No-one wanted the wound reopened or aired publicly for another gruesome round. For many in the community it felt like we had just begun the restoration of trust only to be 'king hit' with the announcement that the school would now become a case study of the royal commission.

In contrast to the current school community, the past students and their families were looking to me for justice, and ultimately, healing. They wanted the wound's dressing ripped off, particularly those past students who had never admitted openly that they had been victims of abuse. While many didn't want to face their past, many did want the opportunity for their voice to be heard at the public hearing. Would I be like those who had gone before me and seek to cover up the allegations to protect the school's reputation? Or would I bring to light the truth of what had happened to them and restore trust?

When trust is destroyed in the workplace, how do you restore it? The pivotal events around the royal commission led me to complete a PhD to identify the specific practices leaders used to enrich a culture of trust. Since then I have had the privilege of running workshops for well over 3000 leaders in the education and corporate worlds, sharing my toolkit of effective strategies in how to become *more trustworthy*. This book outlines the 10 leadership practices for building trust that emerged from my research, and also offers an insight into my first-hand experience of rebuilding trust within an organisation and a school community who felt betrayed. It has been written for leaders from all spheres and has two main purposes.

The first is to highlight the impact that an absence of trust has at an individual and at an organisational level. What happened at the school during the 1980s and 1990s destroyed trust – the foundational building block for human relationships – for countless individuals. At a personal level, lives were indelibly and, in some cases, irreparably changed. This part of the story, while confronting, is important because it should never have occurred. The telling of this story is a poignant reminder that, at its very core, leadership is all about relationships. But the impact of distrust wasn't just on individuals; the events also had a long-lasting impact on the organisation. The story of abuse that occurred at the school is an extreme case of what happens when trust is destroyed, but it isn't an isolated case. The royal commission, and subsequent royal commissions into finance and aged care that followed, uncovered massive failings in a broad range of organisations across the country.

The second purpose of this book is to provide the reader with an insight into trust and what a vital and powerful resource it is. The school where the events occurred has since been listed among the 100 most innovative learning institutions in the world and the Australian School of the Year for 2019. The reason for this? The restoration of trust.

Principled tells the story of trust destroyed and regained and as it does, aims to impart practical advice that can be adopted by any leader wishing to become a *more trustworthy* leader.

INTRODUCTION

WHY TRUST?

In this day and age it would seem that not just two, but three things are certain in life: death, taxes and the decline of trust. In 2017 the Edelman Trust Barometer, the world's most respected measurement of trust, reported the largest-ever decline in trust towards public institutions. Trust in the media, governments, corporate and not-for-profit organisations fell more sharply than ever before. It's little wonder when you consider some of the events of the past few years, with incidents of misconduct increasing and criminal deeds of individuals being exposed.

In 2018 the Australian Royal Commission into Misconduct in the Banking, Superannuation and Financial Services Industry uncovered horrendous practices such as charging dead people for financial advice. For months, the government resisted calls for a royal commission, but those who consistently lobbied for an investigation at the highest level have since been vindicated. As a result, once great and trusted financial institutions, such as AMP, were left in tatters. Financial regulators condemned executives at the company for years of malpractice. The Chairperson, a number of the Directors and the CEO stepped down amid a backlash from shareholders.

The interim findings of the royal commission into banking came as little surprise. It followed another significant royal commission, one that examined institutional responses to child sexual abuse. That Commission handed down a finding of catastrophic failure on the part of the Catholic Church and other churches. Institutions at the heart of our communities, entrusted to care for the marginalised and vulnerable, had been abusing their power and had failed countless people for decades.

It isn't just our foundational institutions that are suffering from massive failures. The 2018 summer cricket season was marred by a ball-tampering scandal that resulted in a 12-month ban for the Australian Captain and Vice-Captain. Then in February the ABC reported that a number of donors to the Australian arm of the international aid organisation Oxfam had withdrawn their financial support in the wake of revelations that senior staff members from Oxfam UK paid local Haiti women for sex. Indeed, the Australian Charities and Not-for-profits Commission reported levels of trust and confidence in charities had fallen from 37 per cent in 2013 to 24 per cent in 2017, and those who have an outright distrust in charities had increased by 4 per cent over the same period.

Australian politics is no better. ABC's Vote Compass survey asks voters to rate our leaders out of 10 on how competent and trustworthy they are. On average, none is getting a passing grade. The 2019 Federal election saw a record number of pre-poll votes cast, probably because citizens are tired of campaigns that seem to be more focused on spreading a doctrine of fear rather than a compelling vision for our nation. The irony of this continuous cycle of political disappointment became evident decades ago when John Howard delivered his 1996 campaign policy speech, in an election he went on to win: 'I think it is important to the future of our country that we rebuild a sense of trust and confidence in words given and commitments made by our political leaders.' Leap forward to 2019 and the CSIRO releases its *Australian National Outlook*, a road map to 2060. Out of the six key challenges the country now faces, number five is trust: in governments, businesses, non-government organisations and the media. As the report states: 'Unless trust can be restored, Australia will find it difficult to build consensus on the long-term solutions required to address the other challenges.'

One could surmise that the demise of once great and trusted institutions is solely an Australian problem, but this is not so. Trump's accession to the White House in 2017 was primarily the result of a lack of trust in his rival on polling day. It wasn't so much a case of victory for Trump as perhaps a loss of faith in his rival. The dearth of leadership is evident the world over, and this is underpinned by a decline in trust.

These issues are amplifying the demand for better leadership, and people have begun specifically to call for 'authentic' leadership. The Australian financial regulator's damning report into the Commonwealth Bank's 'culture and leadership' stated: 'Institutions [should be] focused on developing authentic leadership, "walking the talk" and building open and trusting cultures, to embed a continual concern for safety into the DNA of the organisation.'

Now more than ever, the word 'trust' is being inextricably linked with the word 'leadership'; but although the demand for authentic leadership is rising because of widespread failure by many of our current leaders, it must be acknowledged that *trust* and *leadership* have always been inextricably linked. Churchill had to win the trust of his Cabinet and constituents before he could implement his risky Operation Dynamo evacuation of Dunkirk, pulling off what many since have called a miracle. This, and countless other examples of successful and even inspiring leadership, highlight the importance of trust. Conversely, we could also cite examples of the failure of aspiring leaders who stumbled at the very first hurdle because they failed to win the trust of their followers. These examples come to mind less readily because those leaders are all but forgotten.

No-one wants to follow a person they do not trust. Who wants to board a plane with a pilot who hasn't been issued their licence to fly? Trust is widely recognised as one of the key qualities that a successful leader needs to bring about change within their organisation. Professor Andy Hargreaves, a well-respected researcher, writer, speaker and policy advisor, affirms the value of trust: 'It creates and consolidates energy, commitment and relationships. When trust is broken, people lessen their commitment and withdraw from relationships and entropy abounds.'

The CEO of any organisation, be it for- or not-for-profit, is pivotal in establishing and evolving the culture; culture being the set of social practices and norms that have become the benchmark of what is accepted as common practice. What many organisational heads often fail to appreciate is how profoundly their behaviour as the leader can define these standards for staff. Organisational culture is influenced by many things, but none more so than the CEO's leadership style; the way they motivate direct reports, gather and use information, make decisions, manage change initiatives and handle crises. In fact, according to Daniel Goleman, eminent behavioural scientist and writer for *The New York Times*, leadership styles affect organisational culture by as much as 70 per cent, which in turn leads to a 30 per cent impact on the organisation's performance. Organisational culture is affected by trust and trust can be fostered or diminished by the behaviour of the leader.

WHAT IS TRUST?

The topic of trust is both intriguing and elusive. The idea of trust is hard to define but we certainly know when it is missing. Some have said that we notice trust as we notice air, only when it becomes scarce or polluted. That pollution, or distrust, can cause resentment and frustration, making some people deeply unhappy and unproductive in their work. Betrayal and distrust are particularly insidious behaviours because they easily undermine the mission and objectives of an organisation. When trust is low, most people feel uneasy or apprehensive, or they perceive danger and go into self-protection mode. They personalise everything, using unnecessary energy and precious time to assess the risks in dealing with everyone, constantly worrying that they will be the recipients of others' harmful actions.

In her book *The Truth About Trust in Business*, author Vanessa Hall, also known as the 'Trust Lady', acknowledged the difficulties in defining trust. She interviewed 600 people in the business world about what the word meant and found a stunning 90 per cent of interviewees found it difficult to define. Responses were varied, and included:

'[Trust is] knowing that you can depend on somebody so that they would do what they say they would do: they are reliable.'

'It is just being honest with somebody; you feel safe with them and believe what they say.'

'It means you can depend on someone.'

'[Trust is] having the confidence in the situation or the person you are dealing with that you won't be deceived or misled.'

When Hall asked the respondents to imagine a person that they trusted the most and then list words that came to mind to describe that person, the top five responses were: honesty, genuineness, integrity, selflessness and consistency. In contrast, the top five words people used to describe the person that they trust the least were: dishonesty, selfishness, scheming, incongruence and backstabbing.

Hall also found that 99 per cent agreed that trust was a critical component of a strong relationship, but 95 per cent said that they did not consciously and actively build trust in their organisations. This was certainly true for one of Australia's largest banks. In a 2017 document, published before the Royal Commission into Misconduct in the Banking, Superannuation and Financial Services Industry, Ian Narev, the then CEO of the Commonwealth Bank of Australia (CBA), stated that the company's vision was 'to excel at securing and enhancing the financial wellbeing of people, businesses and communities'. Narev's opening message in that document continued:

Trust is CBA's most important asset. As we strive to achieve our vision, the trust our stakeholders have in us will be strengthened. In turn, this will help us ensure CBA continues as a sustainable and successful organisation. Our stakeholders' trust in us rests on our honesty, capability and genuine concern for their financial wellbeing.

Trust was identified as a key asset by the CEO, but interestingly it wasn't included as one of the company's core values (which at the time were listed as: integrity, accountability, collaboration, excellence and service). The royal commission found that stakeholders' trust in the CBA was, in some cases, severely misplaced with the bank facing findings of misconduct in its lending practices and over its subsidiary, Bankwest, and at least five breaches of the banking code of conduct over conflicted advice and remuneration practices. Part of the CBA's undoing, along with that of the other financial institutions that fell under the royal commission's spotlight, was that they didn't actively attend to building trust in their organisation beyond making tokenistic comments in their mission statements.

Perhaps the best way to understand trust is to recognise that it cannot be accurately defined because it is a socially constructed phenomenon. Social trust exists only when people come together in relationships, not unlike another socially constructed phenomenon: leadership. Currently, there are over 30,000 definitions of leadership because leadership, like trust, means different things to different people. Each of us looks for different types of leadership depending on our view of the world and the situation in which we find ourselves; but above all, we look for leaders we can trust. A person's understanding of trust will depend on the lens of their life experience; the way they view the world because of their past experiences. For example, a person who has had their confidences broken will define trust by that experience. For another, who has experienced the betrayal of an exposed affair, trust will be defined differently. We each value trust and enjoy its benefits without realising it, but we certainly know when it is missing because it causes pain and makes us behave in ways contrary to what we believe and value.

WHY IS TRUST IMPORTANT?

Trust is considered to be the lubricant that makes it possible for
organisations to work. This is because organisations are places
where people come together for a common purpose and where
relationships are formed, albeit for work purposes. When trust
is low or absent, staff may be evasive, dishonest or inconsiderate
in their communications. In the absence of trust, people are
increasingly unwilling to take risks and they demand greater
protections to defend their interests; issues are seldom discussed
and rarely resolved, and people are likely to say only those things
that they expect others will want to hear. It is less likely that a
company will be able to innovate and remain competitive if trust
is low or absent. A low-trust culture can often be the result of,
or result in, the leader resorting to a traditional hierarchical and
authoritarian form of control and leadership. This can in turn
become an endless cycle of distrust, broken only by the removal
of the leader.

Conversely, the rewards of a trusting environment are
immeasurable. Neuroscientist Paul Zak has studied trust and
published several pieces of work on the topic, the most prominent
being his 2017 publication, *Trust Factor: The Science of Creating
High-Performance Companies*. In that work Zak states that people
at high-trust companies report 74 per cent less stress, 106 per
cent more energy at work, 50 per cent higher productivity,
13 per cent fewer sick days, 76 per cent more engagement,
29 per cent more satisfaction with their lives and 40 per cent
less burnout than those at low-trust companies. The effect of
a high-trust environment is likely to manifest in motivated,
satisfied and confident employees. Due to an atmosphere of trust,
employees are more likely to work harder, be optimistic and feel

a heightened sense of professionalism. New ideas are more likely to be generated, creating new opportunities for business.

Without trust, leaders lose credibility. Whether you're the CFO of a big tech firm or the managing partner of a law firm, if your team doesn't find you trustworthy then your credibility is critically damaged, and this will have an impact on your bottom line. The loss of credibility presents a difficulty for leaders as they seek to encourage people to respond to their responsibilities. The painful alternative is to be punitive, seeking to control people through manipulation or coercion.

The building of trust should be the core business of any leader no matter the context: sport, politics, business, not-for-profit, church or voluntary organisations. Once trust is established, it becomes the norm that sets the standard for how employees (both paid and voluntary) behave towards each other and perform their work. Once it becomes part of the culture of an organisation, trust works to liberate people to be their best, to give others their best, and to take risks and innovate.

Thomas Sergiovanni, former professor in leadership and administration at Trinity University and author of the 2005 book *Strengthening the Heartbeat*, says that trust is so important that it is vital to build trust before anything else, even before a leader develops a vision or a strategy for the company. To build trust after setting a vision and developing a strategy is nowhere near as effective. When employees view their leader as trustworthy, a well-communicated vision becomes collective, inspiring commitment on the part of the staff to take the necessary risks and innovative steps required to realise that vision. There is a level of predictability for people when others react and behave in a trusting way; beliefs of acting in good faith abound.

TRUST MYTHS DISPELLED

So, if trust is so important, how do leaders go about nurturing and growing it? This was the key question that faced me after the first six months of my second headship, when I realised I had come into an organisation that was gripped by a culture of distrust and fear, created as a result of the abuse that had occurred at the school and the subsequent attempts by leadership to ensure it never occurred again. Staff demanded that I be trustworthy, but beyond just being honest and a man of integrity how could I, as the leader, grow a culture of trust? The question burned heavily in my mind and heart. The weight of responsibility for the organisation became heavier as I learnt about how the historical abuse, and subsequent denials, had impacted upon the way people worked.

Recognising that it was my primary responsibility to improve workplace culture, I wanted to know how I could best be using my time to build and develop trust. The question led me to several years of reading, reflecting and watching other leaders in their work. It finally gave birth to a doctoral study to understand how I could be a more effective leader. My research began with the identification of four highly trusted transformational leaders who led large and successful organisations. Those leaders were then studied in context; their employees were interviewed, along with the chairs of their governing bodies. This data was then triangulated before a cross-case analysis of each leader was undertaken. The results were four fascinating, myth-busting findings.

Firstly, *leadership trust is not dependent on personality*. Each of the leaders studied had their own individual personality traits and idiosyncrasies. Two were introverts who had a clear boundary between professional and personal, and two were extroverts who tended to blur that boundary. Two of the four people had to work very hard on their interpersonal skills while the other two found interacting with people natural. Three of the four had a deep sense of care and compassion for people while the other valued professionalism above being *liked*. One of the leaders said to me, 'Trust isn't about being nice, because I'm certainly not nice,' and she was right; first impressions of this leader were intimidating. The results of the study showed that trust in a leader was not dependent on personal attributes or an individual's ability to develop relationships. It was all about how they acted or behaved as a leader. This was a pertinent finding as it clearly indicated that trust was a leadership practice that anyone could learn and develop.

The second interesting thing that came out of the study was that *trust is not built over time.* We often think of trust as something we grow, like a bank account from which we can then make a withdrawal. The study showed this not to be the case. One of the leaders studied had been at their current organisation for just one year; another had been there for 17 years. The findings showed that it wasn't a question of whether or not you are trusted, but how much you are trusted; and the amount of trust afforded to you was solely dependent on how you led, not on how long people had known you: actions speak louder than words.

The third finding was that *trust and transformational leadership are indelibly linked.* Transformational leadership is the leader's ability to realise a vision for the organisation, to transform it from its current form to something different and better in the future: to innovate. The study proved what others had wisely said before it: that you cannot achieve a vision without first having the trust of those you are asking to tread boldly into the unknown beside and behind you.

The final finding was that *each of the leaders was employing multiple practices to engender trust.* The study differed from many others in that it examined the concept of trust from the perspective of the people who offered it to the leader: the employees. They had been aware of the purpose of my research for several weeks before I arrived to gather the data. This provided participants with the chance to reflect on the behaviour of their leader. Many came to the interview with notes in readiness to share.

The opening question of each interview was a request for the participant to articulate their understanding of trust. As Vanessa Hall found when she undertook a study into the meaning of trust, the understanding of the concept differed considerably from participant to participant. This in turn impacted on the identification of the practices that were important for each employee. Their responses to my interview questions included:

'Trust is knowing that the person is there to support you and that you can count on them. Someone you can go to if you need help – [I trust my employer because] he stood by me on an issue with a member of staff; that really meant a lot to me.'

'Trust would be to allow someone to use their own initiative, their own judgement, to follow through on something without stepping in and coming over the top of them to say, "Do it this way." I trust her because she trusts me – she doesn't come in over the top of my department and tell me what to do. She has put me in charge of it and she lets me be in charge of it.'

As each person has their own life experience and understanding of the concept of trust, it follows that no single leadership practice will engender the collective trust of an entire staff. One practice may be of value to one person but have no value to another. To engender the trust of a greater number of people a leader must therefore employ a range of practices.

The four leaders who were the focus of the study each employed between 11 and 15 practices. However, while evidence suggests that a range of practices should be employed, using a greater number of practices does not necessarily result in higher levels of trust. Indeed, the most trusted CEO employed 12 practices to engender trust, while the fourth most trusted leader used 15. It could not be concluded from the study how many or which practices are more important, or which combinations of practices have greater impact on the generation of trust. However, when a cross-case analysis was undertaken it revealed 10 key practices that were common to highly trusted leaders (see Figure 1.1)

TRUST-BUILDING PRACTICE	DESCRIPTION WHEN DONE WELL
Listening	Listens far more than they speak without distraction; asks clarifying questions; demonstrates empathy and can succinctly summarise what the person is feeling and values.
Admitting Mistakes	Displays professional and personal vulnerability; has the humility and strength of character to admit their mistakes and actively rectifies the problems; willingly takes responsibility for others' mistakes.
Offering Trust	Treats employees as professional colleagues by trusting them to perform their roles; provides coaching or mentoring to grow the careers of others.

Consultative Decision-Making	Uses a consultative decision-making process to value employee's views and opinions; makes timely and informed decisions and enacts them.
Providing Affirmation	Actively seeks ways to affirm and recognise employees; looks for ways to thank staff for the difference that they have made.
Visibility	Is regularly seen by staff around the organisation; interacts with employees, customers and stakeholders; is accessible to everyone.
Demeanour	Is consistent and predictable in their demeanour; always remains calm and level-headed no matter the situation; is always respectful of others, no matter their position or background.
Coaching or Mentoring	Maximises employees' potential and career growth by personally investing in them; provides immediate, specific feedback that promotes continued growth and development.
Caring	Extends a genuinely benevolent concern for members of the team; invests time to get to know individual employees as people; offers practical support.
Keeping Confidences	Keeps the confidences of employees when they are entrusted with sensitive information; acts on information only with permission.

Figure 1.1

The following chapters each deal with one of the 10 key trust-building practices – what they look like when they are working effectively, and what they look like at their worst. My research suggests that it isn't a question of whether or not a person is trusted, but rather a question of how much they are trusted. This stands to reason: we expect people to automatically offer us their full trust while we withhold offering it ourselves, perhaps offering it in degrees depending on how well we know a person or what our life story has been.

A parent, for example, might trust an eight-year-old with $10, but perhaps not $100 until they have proven themselves as responsible. Every leader will be adept at each of the 10 practices somewhere on a continuum between poor and highly accomplished. The descriptions of the practice *when it is working* and *when it isn't working* will help you reflect on your own trust-building actions.

A reflection of each practice is drawn from my first-hand experience as a leader. These reflections not only illustrate an example of the practice in action but help to provide an understanding of what happens when trust is destroyed in a person and an organisation, and ultimately how it can be restored.

The aim of the following chapters is to help you to move further along the continuum of each of the practices to become *more trustworthy*. To support that journey, the final part of each chapter contains a list of tips to help hone your skills to get better at the art of leadership with a focus on creating a culture of trust.

10 PRACTICES THAT BUILD TRUST

Practice *noun*, a habit or custom; repeated performance or systematic exercise for the purpose of acquiring skill or proficiency; the action or process of doing something.

Trust *noun*, indefinable, but relationships only work when mutual trust and respect exists.

#1. LISTENING

'If one gives an answer before he hears, it is his folly and shame.'

— Proverbs 18:13

I enjoy listening to music. I have quite a number of favourite songs but I couldn't tell you the lyrics to any of them. It amazes me when I come across people who know all the lyrics to their favourite songs; a reflection perhaps, on my listening skills? I listen but I don't necessarily hear.

I do struggle to listen well. I often find myself switching off, my mind wandering on to other things. An idea might pop into my head, and in desperation not to forget it, I focus on that idea rather than the person who is sharing their thoughts and feelings with me. My body language probably tells it all. People might see my eyes glaze over, a vacant look taking the place of a once attentive expression.

While I struggle to listen well, I do want others to listen to me when I have something to share. I can tell when someone isn't interested in what I have to say, or interested in me as a person. I know when they aren't giving me their undivided attention: they spend more time speaking, offering me advice, or telling me about the time when …

How many people genuinely listen? For most people, listening is part of a bigger act, the act of conversation. Because many people see listening as just a small part of the act of conversation their listening skills are marginalised. They listen for the flow of the conversation, the topic, the points of view being shared, waiting for a break so they can add their opinion. Far too often the skill of listening is never nurtured and grown beyond waiting for our own turn to speak.

Talking is easy. Listening is hard work. Talking is simply verbalising the thoughts in our brain, whereas to listen, we have to work hard to clear all those thoughts from our mind and focus on the present, the person in front of us.

Listening is not about you; it is about connecting with the other person on a level far deeper than the superficial. In recent years, there has been a move to add an adjective to describe different types of listening as though there has been some sort of new discovery about the act. 'Active listening' is described as a communication technique that requires the listener to understand and interpret what they hear. The approach encourages you to suspend your judgement so you are fully attentive to the speaker. I find it odd that we should describe listening with different adjectives or adverbs. Surely listening is listening, either done poorly, done well, or somewhere in between. However, what was clearly evident from my research is that listening, when done well, builds trust.

WHEN IT ISN'T WORKING

Nothing is more frustrating when you are trying to express how you feel than when a person who is meant to be listening to you constantly interrupts, jumping in to share their experience, finish your sentences or offer advice. It is just as discouraging when they are distracted, staring off into the distance or looking over your shoulder for someone more interesting to engage with. What they are conveying by their inattentiveness is that you don't matter to them, that you're not as smart or wise as them and that they don't really have time for you.

When people don't feel listened to, anger can fill the void that should have been filled with empathy. There is not just a lack of connection, but the speaker is often left with feelings of disappointment. These feelings run the risk of manifesting themselves as irritation, annoyance and even rage. As reported from participants in my own research into trust:

'He/she doesn't care enough to truly understand how I feel.'

'What is the good of speaking to him/her because they won't listen, nothing will change.'

Most people don't share deeply personal experiences and feelings with you because they want you to do something about them. They are sharing because they want someone to empathise with what they are thinking or feeling. They want to be believed. Poor listening doesn't bear that fruit. No connection occurs and, as a result, the speaker is left feeling undervalued, marginalised and powerless. As a consequence, any trust they had in you is diminished, or even destroyed.

WHEN IT IS WORKING

Nothing is quite as reassuring or comforting as feeling that someone is properly listening to you. It is a gift of compassion and empathy when a person is totally present for us, fully engaged, giving us their undivided attention: earnestly seeking to understand who we truly are. Listening is at its best when preconceptions are put aside and no bias or judgement is brought to bear on what is being said. This is not an easy thing to do. As humans we are continually assessing other people and situations. It is part of our 'fight or flight' instinct. We are forming judgements about who a person is and what their motivations might be. Unless we have the skill and the mindfulness to set these preconceptions aside, they will taint the listening process: we will be subconsciously looking for evidence to support our initial judgements, and building a case that reinforces our version of the truth. This is why listening is such hard work, a deliberate act of will.

Good listeners speak for less than 20 per cent of the conversation. As Stephen Covey said in his 2006 book *The Speed of Trust*, 'seek first to understand … then to be understood'. Over the years, I have learnt to minimise what I say. As the leader I don't have to have all the answers. Great listeners rarely speak, something I have had to work really hard at. When they do they are primarily asking clarifying questions to gain a better understanding of what the person has said, or to summarise what they have heard, identifying the emotions the person has tried to express.

Good listeners look for the emotions a person is expressing. Great listeners look for what the person *values*. Values cut to the heart of our identity. They define and control our actions. For example, if I value collaboration I would behave in ways that are different from how I would if I didn't value working with others. Or, if I really value my relationship with another person I would act in ways that avoid diminishing that relationship. What a person values is manifest in their emotions, and then their reaction to various events and experiences; that is, the person's behaviours.

When speaking aloud a person will rarely verbalise what they value, but it will be implied in their choice of language, the expression of their emotions, and even in their body language. Great listeners have the ability to identify what the speaker values and reflect that back to them for clarification. If they are able to do this then they will have truly sought to understand what is being said and will connect on a deeper level, not only showing how much they value that person as a fellow human being, but also demonstrating how trustworthy they are.

When we truly listen we are not just suspending our preconceptions about a situation or refraining from making a judgement, we are exposing ourselves to a particular vulnerability. We are putting at risk our own preconceptions of the world, our own beliefs and our own values.

In *Becoming a Person*, American psychologist Carl Rogers wrote:

If you really understand another person, if you are willing to enter his private world and see the way life appears to him, without any attempt to make evaluative judgements, you run the risk of being changed yourself. You might see it his way, you might find yourself influenced in your attitudes … The risk of being changed is one of the most frightening prospects most of us face.

Perhaps my most profound learning about building trust has been to realise the healing power of listening. It is an enormous privilege when people share their story with you. To truly listen to another person is to put your existing beliefs at risk. What if the other person is right? What if I have to change my mind? What if I have no answer to give, or I have to admit I have made a mistake?

REFLECTION

In 2013, Prime Minister Julia Gillard established the Royal Commission into Institutional Responses to Child Sexual Abuse, following revelations that child abusers moved from place to place without their crimes being reported, and revelations that countless adults failed to stop these heinous acts from occurring. The royal commission gave a voice to the victims of sexual abuse and shed light on the poor practices of churches, schools, children's homes and other groups entrusted with the care of young people.

The organisation I led became a case study at the royal commission because of the complexity of the crimes committed at the school and the number of students who suffered. Two abusers were identified in the case study, a music teacher who was employed during the early 1980s and a school counsellor who was on the staff from 1989 to 1997. He had come from another non-government school working in a similar role. Over 200 victims of those two paedophiles came forward to share their stories. It is suspected that there are many more.

Appointed to the school as its fourth headmaster in 2008, well after the crimes were committed, I was called to the hearing to provide evidence. The procedure shed light on the school and brought forward known, and new, victims. The floodgates were opened and there was an outpouring of anger and grief, expressed in the courtroom, in the media, and in my office. For three months following the public hearing I met with, listened to on the telephone, or received emails or letters from three or four victims a day, seven days a week.

In the weeks prior to the hearing one past student, Archie, gave his testimony on a blog page. It was the first time he had disclosed to the public that he had been abused as a vulnerable young boy. His testimony was graphic and horrific. His rage was palpable. Followers of his blog waited with bated breath to see what the next allegation might be, and whom he was going to implicate in the crimes. The lawyers in the courtroom were also watching. Archie's story had not only caught their intrigue, but their concern. What new evidence would Archie offer and who might he put in the frame next?

In the end there was no time to provide my evidence in the hearing, but as the current headmaster I was given the opportunity to express how deeply sorry I was for what had happened. I wanted to explain that things had changed, and to assure the victims, the Commission and the wider community, that we were committed to protecting the children entrusted to our care. The hearing was streamed live and Archie watched from afar. Much to everyone's surprise, Archie acknowledged and accepted the apology and the atmosphere in the courtroom subsequently changed.

Then one day in February, four months after the hearing, Archie turned up at the school. He hadn't set foot on school grounds since leaving in 1984, the pain and anger he had felt being too great to face. He came because there was a beginning of trust. For the first time he felt like he had been heard, he had been believed, and he had been apologised to.

It took three months of emailing back and forth before Archie agreed to meet with me. You can listen when someone is speaking in the written form. You can do this by reflecting back what you have heard and acknowledging the person's perspective. While it is harder than listening in person, it is not impossible. I learnt to listen carefully. My responses to Archie always acknowledged his pain. As hard as it was, I had to suspend judgement and not react, or jump to the defence of the organisation I headed. A person is far more valuable and important than an organisation's reputation.

Gradually, over the course of weeks and months Archie shared his story. Initially I was confronted, and a little fearful of how angry and bitter he was. I had never heard or seen the impact of such trauma. But by taking the time to listen to Archie I realised that my first impressions had been wrong. After listening to Archie I discovered that despite first impressions, he really valued truth and justice. He valued family, his parents, and relationships. These values were driving his actions, his emotions, and his pursuit of the truth behind events that occurred at the school.

The act of listening to Archie, and to countless others, changed me. I began to see past the preconceptions I had of victims who were drug addicts, who have done time and were now living on the streets, people who I had previously judged as being a lesser person than I was. I began to see past the irate parent in my office who was viciously defending their child, justifying their inappropriate behaviour, blaming me for making the 'wrong decision'.

Through that journey with Archie, I learnt how important it was for me as a leader to listen more, and better. I needed first to understand Archie's values – what was driving his behaviour and motivating his actions – in order to develop empathy. As I listened, I started to see a person wounded by trauma. A person who had their childhood and innocence robbed from them. A person who was filled with rage and hate instead of happiness and joy, not because of what I had said or done, but because of what had happened to him when he was growing up. I began to see a person who just wanted to be believed, to be accepted, and to be valued as an equal.

Good leadership is about effectively managing relationships, and one of the most effective ways of doing this is to improve your listening skills. Through my experience with Archie I discovered that the greatest leadership challenge at the school was not what I would have expected as an educator. My greatest challenge was to heal the past. Listening to Archie, and others like him, had three powerful effects. It changed me as a person; I stopped judging others and saw people in a different light – as people damaged by trauma. Listening began the healing process for the victims; they began to let go of their anger and started to return to the school. Some even chose to enrol their children because they believed once again in the goodness of others. Finally, reconciliation with the past student community relieved the current staff of a heavy burden they (unfairly) felt. Many had felt blame, that they should have known and done something to protect the children. They could now move forward knowing that confidence in the organisation had been restored.

GETTING BETTER

We hear, but we often don't actually listen. This is certainly true for me. As a CEO my time is very precious. My diary is full and there is a huge number of demands placed on my time. Yet I was confronted one day when a staff member bravely stopped what she was saying to me and, changing the tone of her voice said: 'Paul, I can see that you're not listening to me. Have you heard anything I have tried to tell you?'

Listening is hard. It is a skill; with effort and practice you can get better. Here are some suggestions for how you can improve your listening skills:

Minimise distractions If you are like me, your mind will be going at a million miles an hour, constantly thinking of ideas or things that need to be done. All the 'other' things happening around me can be distracting. If this sounds like you, then you need to minimise those distractions that take you away from being truly present with the person you are seeking to understand. Turn your mobile onto silent. Take the landline off the hook. My desktop makes an audible alert each time an email comes in. Turn that sound off if it causes your mind to wander. Think about where you will sit. Don't seat yourself within view of your computer screen, or near a window so you can see what is happening outside your office – these will offer further distractions and mean you break eye contact. And on that note, think about the comfort of the person you are talking to; make sure that the sun isn't in their eyes and that there isn't something physical between you, like a desk, that can create a barrier.

Understand body language When we really listen to someone it is not just to the words that are being spoken but the way they are being presented. Watch the person intently as they are speaking. Their body language will give you lots of clues as to what they are really trying to say: the person's posture, gestures (including touch), eye movements, facial expressions, the pace of speech and tone of voice all give you an indication of their mood and intentions. Does the person have a nervous rash on their neck? Are their fists clenching while they are describing an incident? Are they sitting comfortably and relaxed, or are they leaning forward anxiously?

When we really seek to empathise with a person, we subconsciously mimic their body language. We lean forward when they do, fold our arms, tilt our head in the same direction, sit back in our seats and relax when they relax. We have no intention of seeking to truly understand or listen to another person if we aren't mimicking their body language. Being conscious of this intuitive mimicking behaviour will help you focus better on the person you are listening to rather than getting lost in thought about your next appointment.

Make eye contact Humans communicate most effectively in person, and when they are making eye contact. Not looking at someone while they are speaking conveys a lack of interest. However, take care not to stare; gazing into one eye for lengthy periods of time can arouse feelings of anxiety. If you are sensing a person is becoming uncomfortable, move your gaze in a triangular pattern from one eye to the other and then to their mouth, changing your focus every five seconds.

Look for emotion The real skill in listening is to hear the story behind the story. This story can be found, in part, in the emotions of the person speaking. A raised voice, a hint of sadness or frustration – tone of voice and body language all provide hints about how the person is feeling. When you understand the emotions that are driving their expression, then you have begun to truly understand them and develop empathy by entering their world.

Listen for the values What I hadn't realised until I attended an intense coaching course with the Center for Creative Leadership in Singapore, was the power of listening for a person's values. Most people won't tell you directly what they value, but if you listen hard to their choice of words and their non-verbal emotional cues you will be able to understand what is important to them, and it is these values that will manifest in the person's behaviours and actions. For example, if a person is expressing their frustration with a colleague, or is annoyed with a team member, it may be because they value collaboration and the situation they have been in isn't allowing them to collaborate. When you understand a person's values, you will have really connected with them and they will feel understood. There are few greater gifts you can offer a person than to demonstrate genuine understanding.

Take notes The skill of listening takes effort, far more than speaking. Taking notes while a person is talking can help you stay focused in the present. In formal settings people won't mind if you take notes when you meet with them. It is polite to state up front what you are doing and check that they are okay with it. This has a two-fold benefit: it declares your intentions, sending the message that you value what the person is saying enough to make notes, and it helps you remain focused. Record not just the facts and opinions, but also the emotions the person is expressing and the values you think they hold.

Suspend judgement This is something I struggle with. Before a person even begins to speak I have already formed a judgement about them or the situation. As they speak, I am looking for evidence to support my judgement. When this happens I don't enter the act of listening with the intent to understand; instead, I enter the conversation to prove that I am right.

As Doctor Edith Eger writes in her memoir, *The Choice*, about surviving the holocaust: 'Find the bigot in you ... and exorcise it.' The purpose of listening is to understand another person as if you were in their shoes, not to make a judgement about them or assign labels. Truth is often a perspective. What is true for you will be different for me, or the next person.

Your job when listening is to understand what the truth looks like from the other person's perspective of the world. As challenging as it is, particularly if you know the person, or if they have a reputation in the community, you have to suspend your judgement. Listen as though it is the first time you have met the person and you are just starting on a journey of getting to know them.

Resist the urge to give advice Good listeners speak for no more than 20 per cent of the time, and most of that 20 per cent is to ask clarifying questions or to reflect back to the speaker what they think they have heard. This is particularly hard, especially if you are an extrovert, you are in a hurry, or you think you already know exactly what needs to happen to fix the problem or find a solution.

However, when we interrupt people to offer advice, we start making the situation about us, and not the other person. Nine times out of 10, the person just wants to share their story, they aren't looking for advice; nor do they want to know that you can empathise with or have sympathy for them. While you may have had a similar experience, the moment you share this you are again starting to make the act about you. Listening at its best is a selfless act. It is about the other person and not you. It is about entering their world and seeing it from their viewpoint.

Reflect back for clarification and affirmation As you are listening, you will be making assumptions about what you have heard. Those assumptions will not just be about the facts and opinions a person is telling you, but also about the underlying emotions connected to the story and the values that person holds.

Good listeners reflect back for clarification by asking specific questions about all the information they have heard and gathered. For example: 'I really want to understand you and so I just want to check that I have heard you properly. I could sense your frustration as you were telling me about the situation. I can hear that you really value collaboration but you haven't had the opportunity to do that.'

The tone of voice you use will indicate that you are seeking clarification or affirmation. This aspect of listening also has a two-fold purpose: it checks that you have truly heard and in turn helps you get better information; and it shows the person that you have really understood them or you are trying hard to do so.

When you are asking for clarification, make sure you save your questions until the person has finished speaking. In her 2018 book *An Ordinary Day*, Leigh Sales quoted award-winning journalist Dr Amanda Gearing about the importance of not interrupting traumatised disaster survivors during a narrative: 'As I listened back to the recordings [of my interviews] to transcribe them . . . I heard myself butt in with a question.' These interruptions broke the thread of the story and interviewees struggled to find their place in their narrative. As a result of this finding, Amanda changed the way she interviewed people who had been traumatised. She tried asking an initial question about what had happened and listened to their entire narrative without asking questions, but maintained eye contact, until the person had given their whole account of the event. When she asked questions at the end, she found that interviewees were able to cope with speaking about very confronting material without feeling overwhelmed. This dedication to listening to the whole story without interrupting, and saving questions for the end, is an important skill that honours the speaker.

Keep it timely There is nothing more off-putting than a person who is meant to be listening but checks their watch all the time. If time is a problem and you don't want to be disrespectful, there are a couple of tricks that can help. You could strategically place a clock on the shelf behind the seat of the person you are meeting so you can see the time without giving the appearance of 'keeping an eye on the clock', or you can have your phone on silent. I have my phone set to vibrate 15 minutes before my next appointment, that way I know how much more time I have to listen without having to check.

#2. ADMITTING MISTAKES

'To apologise sincerely is to imply that I am secure enough in my sense of myself to admit I was wrong.'
— Hugh Mackay

History records many famous quotes. This one marked the beginning of a decline of trust in American President Bill Clinton in 1998: 'I want to say one thing to the American people. I want you to listen to me. I'm going to say this again: I did not have sexual relations with that woman, Miss Lewinsky. I never told anybody a lie, not a single time; never.'

Current affairs programs make a living out of exposing companies and individuals for the mistakes they make. Their investigative reporters thrive on telling stories about people's faults and their subsequent impact on the vulnerable and innocent. The advent of social media has enabled the instant communication of a person's fall from grace, often told from one perspective in 140 characters or less. An individual's reputation can be destroyed in an instant.

Likewise, small and big business is not immune to reputational damage and often find themselves in the firing line. This was illustrated in 1982 when Johnson & Johnson found itself in a situation that brought the company's brand into question, seriously impacting its bottom line. When 12-year-old Mary Kellerman woke with a headache she complained to her mother who gave her some paracetamol to relieve the pain. Tragically, within hours, Mary was pronounced dead. Later that day, Adam Janus died in hospital; at first the reason was inexplicable. Five more people died over the next few days. All had taken Tylenol-branded paracetamol capsules manufactured by the multinational's pharmaceutical arm.

Investigations into the incidents revealed that someone had tampered with an unknown number of Tylenol bottles, replacing capsules with potassium cyanide. Johnson & Johnson's response to the incident was ultimately hailed as an exemplary public relations exercise. While the incident was not the fault of the organisation, they chose immediately to recall all Tylenol products. Corporate leaders set up a hotline for consumers. They worked with the FBI, the media and the public to communicate everything that they knew. Even though this resulted in their market-share collapsing from 35 per cent to 8 per cent almost overnight, this didn't deter the top executives from doing what they saw as the right thing. They immediately got to work and within six months the company re-released Tylenol, but this time in a new tamper-proof package and container. All of their actions ultimately strengthened the Johnson & Johnson brand.

The litigious environment in which we live makes it even more difficult for people to admit when they are wrong; the stakes are often extremely high. Those stakes are driven in part by our western legal system. Lawyers regularly advise their clients not to admit culpability lest they should accept the liability of their mistakes. The legal system often appears to be more about protecting wrongdoers and minimising compensation claims, than finding the truth. This is one of the reasons that it is rare for a person or company to utter the simple words, 'I'm sorry'. No-one wants to be wrong. Admitting error is always difficult.

Another reason for our regular failure to admit our mistakes is our innate sense of loyalty, which can skew our view of what is the right thing to do. Our desire to belong and be valued drives a strong sense of loyalty, which sees us quickly move to a particular default position when a mistake is made, to protect the reputation of the company and ourselves at all costs. There is often a perception that there is too much at risk. If we acknowledge error, then there will be consequences to bear, and those costs might be far too great. We first learnt to lie when our parents asked who it was that took the treats from the jar without permission, or who started the fight with our sibling. The fear of negative consequences can easily override our integrity. However, if we are on the other side of a mistake we are the victims of the error, and all we want is justice.

It is important to remember that leaders are not infallible. They haven't been appointed to the role because they live error-free lives. We are all human and can fall foul of our emotions, particularly fear. We are all products of our life experiences, and if we are not careful, the memories of those prior experiences will shape how we respond in the present. But we always have choices, and how leaders deal with their mistakes sets the tone for the rest of the organisation and is a key factor in the creation of trust.

The willingness to be vulnerable, the ability to be self-reflective and recognise one's own strengths and weaknesses, to apologise when an error has been made or reverse a poor decision, exemplifies a leader's humility. This was evidenced in my research into trust and leadership, with one employee describing her CEO's character.

'He is very human; he displays a human error side of him … He is happy to admit when he makes mistakes.'

John Dickson, respected historian and theologian at Sydney University and founder of the Centre for Public Christianity describes humility in leadership as the ability to redirect your power, to forgo your status and deploy your resources or use your influence, for the good of others before yourself. Jim Collins, author of the best-selling book *Good to Great*, asserts that it is possible to be humble, iron-willed and successful – and many successful leaders have these qualities. Employees view this not as a weakness but as a key strength of leadership, connecting them to their leader on a very human level.

'Often she says when she finds [something] a problem, she doesn't always have to know the answer, or be right; she will often express when she is confused about the way forward.'

A leader's willingness to display their vulnerabilities, both personally and professionally, engenders employee admiration and trust.

WHEN IT ISN'T WORKING

At its poorest, a failure to admit mistakes looks like arrogance or even narcissism. Everyone knows a mistake has been made but the leader digs their heels in and continues on regardless. They can't be told, and they can't ever apologise. In their mind, apologising is a sign of weakness. If a response needs to be given, blame is always attributed to someone else, or an excuse is made in a bid to deflect responsibility and even to gain some sympathy from others: 'It wasn't my fault … I am a victim just like you.'

A failure to admit mistakes impacts on the way people work. They in turn keep information to themselves for fear of being blamed for other people's errors. Organisational cultural norms are established with a 'don't tell' mentality, which promotes a culture that values protecting the reputation of the company at all costs. In organisational cultures under this kind of leadership, failure isn't an option and the perception of the risks at stake can be blown out of proportion. As people become more and more protective, further mistakes are made. This is because over time collaboration becomes less and less valued, and fewer people are willing to wear the wrath of the leader when something goes wrong. Under these conditions, innovation will likely never occur. While innovation can often follow on the heels of a crisis, it will only be successful if people are willing to accept responsibility and commit to fixing the problem; that is, when a culture of trust is restored.

WHEN IT IS WORKING

There are many reasons that mistakes are made: not enough information to make the best decision; a lack of time for a proper consultation; a genuine oversight; or a lack of experience are but a few examples. With the pressures of everyday leadership, coupled with the inevitable crises, mistakes will be innocently, accidentally, or at worst, deliberately made. Whatever the reason, mistakes happen.

Humility isn't about being another person's scapegoat, or about being weak. It takes a tremendous strength of character to display vulnerability and admit error. At its best the practice of admitting mistakes will see a leader take responsibility not just for their own faults, but also the mistakes of their employees. They realise that ultimately the accountability for the organisation rests on their shoulders and they are able to put aside their ego and willingly place their own position at risk. They are capable of apologising publicly, either with a verbal or written statement, or both. Following that, they enact a plan to rectify the problem and communicate with all the stakeholders the actions that are being taken to repair the wrong.

All these actions need to occur in a timely fashion, as close as possible to when the mistake was made or discovered, and not after a period of time that could be construed as a misguided hope that no-one will find out, or at worst, as an attempted cover-up. Great leaders know it is better to be on the front foot rather than reactive. They realise that conspiracy theories will fill the void created by inaction. At best, a highly trusted leader will take responsibility and admit their mistakes even when no-one knew that something was wrong. This breeds a culture of ownership, collaboration, responsibility and willingness to take the necessary risks to be innovative. Trust is placed in a person's humanity and not in some kind of misguided superhero status.

REFLECTION

As the headmaster of a school that became a case study in the Royal Commission into Institutional Responses to Child Sexual Abuse I was required to oversee the retrieval of over

100,000 pieces of evidence in readiness for the hearing. This work took the best part of two years. I had been made aware of the abuse when I was first appointed to the leadership of the school. During my first five years as headmaster every now and then a new victim would come forward, either directly to the school or through a solicitor, seeking compensation. This gave me an insight into why the culture of the organisation was as it was, but I really didn't appreciate the gravity of the impact until I began reading the victim impact statements provided to the hearing and subsequently meeting with individual victims to offer them an apology.

During the 1990s, a number of boys claimed they spoke to their school principal, telling him that the school counsellor was acting inappropriately. They said that the counsellor had asked them to take off their pants while he indecently assaulted them. They claimed the principal refused to believe the boys, choosing instead to admonish them, and in some cases, threatened to take away their scholarship if they dared to slander a respectable member of the staff again.

For many who were impacted by the crimes, the response of the principal of the school at the time appeared to be about protecting the reputation of the institution. Several possibilities for this response have since been proposed by victims and their families: he was totally naive and took the word of the counsellor over the young boys'; he knew what was happening at the time and was complicit in the crimes; or, for the sake of a few individuals, it was easiest to sweep the crimes under the carpet, hoping that the media wouldn't get hold of the story. Presumably, the perception of any misconduct at the school would inadvertently reflect on him as the principal and he feared losing his reputation, his position, or both.

Whatever the reason, the principal's response amplified the impact of the abuse for the victims and their families, as they also faced the indignity of being ignored and devalued. Their cries for help were not heard. All they really wanted was to be believed, for someone to acknowledge their pain, and to stop it from happening to others.

Over time that suppressed anger grew. Finally, the abuse became public when in 2000 former Brisbane Grammar School student Nigel Parodi went on a violent rampage and ambushed three policemen, firing 12 bullets from a .22 calibre rifle at close range while the officers were sitting in their vehicle. Experts said that a combination of low-velocity ammunition, a sawn-off rifle and a silencer meant that miraculously, the three officers escaped with their lives. A state-wide manhunt was sparked. The then Queensland Police Commissioner said he would leave no stone unturned in finding 'the self-professed Jesse James.' Parodi's body was found three weeks later in bushland. He had suffered a single gunshot wound to the head. The coroner concluded that he had taken his own life.

Several days later a friend of the gunman came forward, a classmate from his school days, alleging that as a boy Parodi had been abused for two years. The man who abused him would later become school counsellor at St Paul's and abuse over 120 boys. This incident became a focus for Task Force Argos, a branch of the Queensland Police Service founded in 1997. The case opened the first floodgate – dozens of former students banded together, launching civil action against the school and its owner, seeking more than $18 million in damages.

Under new leadership and determined to make amends, the church launched its own inquiry led by Mr Peter O'Callaghan QC and Professor Freda Briggs. On 1 May 2003 O'Callaghan and

Briggs tabled their 471-page report in State Parliament. A seminal quote from that report stated: 'With the ruthlessness and amorality of the paedophile, he took cruel advantage of his position of trust.'

The findings of the report brought renewed pressure against the then Governor-General, Dr Peter Hollingworth. He had been the Archbishop of Brisbane when the abuse at the school occurred. There was a public outcry about his mishandling of abuse cases across the Diocese of Brisbane. There were calls made to the prime minister, asking for Hollingworth to be removed from office. Not long after, he stepped down from his position. In a public statement Hollingworth said:

'Despite the misplaced and unwarranted allegations made against me as governor-general, it is clear that continuing public controversy [around my handling of abuse in the Diocese of Brisbane] has the potential to undermine and diminish my capacity to uphold the importance, dignity and integrity of this high office that I have been privileged and proud to occupy.'

However, it took another 12 years and a royal commission for Hollingworth to publicly make an apology:

'My apology is offered to the children, now adults, and the families of those who have been abused. It is offered to all of you who have suffered great pain and become disillusioned that your complaints were not dealt with from the outset as they should have been ... I deeply regret that I did not press harder to have your complaints investigated more rigorously ... It is clear to me now that we did not do enough to help you, and the actions of the diocese and the school compounded your distress and suffering, and for that I am very sorry.'

It isn't an exaggeration to say that those in the courtroom didn't receive Hollingworth's belated apology well. The truth was that the school did not have adequate protections in place at the time of the abuse. There were no policies or procedures to protect vulnerable children when they attended the school in the 1980s and 1990s. The prevailing culture was that children were to be seen and not heard. The cries of those boys were not listened to, nor were the warning signs recognised. As a result, the school counsellor had unfettered access to dozens of boys. His actions went undetected for decades. The impact of the crimes inflicted on those boys has led to a lifetime of trauma for the victims.

Why did it take Hollingworth so long to admit his role in the failings of the school? Admitting fault takes enormous courage and carries significant risk. The risks are all the greater if you are a public figure – it's a long way to fall. A belated apology, or worse, an apology given because there is no alternative, will rarely be seen as genuine.

As the current headmaster I had no hand in what had gone on in the past. The blame didn't sit with me. But leadership isn't about me, it is about accepting responsibility for a community or an organisation no matter what that may mean or cost. Prime Minister Kevin Rudd (2007–10, 2013) wasn't responsible for the policies of the past that resulted in the removal of thousands of Aboriginal and Torres Strait Islander children from their parents, who later became known as the 'stolen generation.' But none the less, the wrongs of the past needed to be righted.

As one of Kevin Rudd's greatest achievements, on 13 February 2008 he publicly accepted responsibility and apologised.

The victims and their families knew I wasn't to blame for the abuse that occurred at the school but their anger was, in part, directed at the organisation I now led. They needed to know that their school accepted responsibility, that it, at last, believed their cries, and would assure that future children would be protected no matter the cost. As the current headmaster I needed to take responsibility and publicly acknowledge the failings of the past and apologise for them.

While the church inquiry led to the acknowledgement that crimes had occurred and to the establishment of a compensation scheme for victims, it took another decade for the owners of St Paul's to finally acknowledge the impact on the parents of the boys. In what was a controversial decision, school fees paid to attend the school were to be refunded to the mothers and fathers of victims.

This decision was announced during the public hearing of the royal commission by the current archbishop, and was gratefully accepted by the victims and their families. However, concerned the precedent would open the floodgates for further litigation, the decision wasn't welcomed by other private schools around the country facing similar problems. At the time of writing those schools still refuse the pleas of their ex-students to follow suit and acknowledge the damage.

GETTING BETTER

Perhaps there is no harder thing to do than to admit that we are wrong, or that a mistake has been made, but the ability to apologise and make amends is a key trust-building action, and not a sign of weakness. The following practical steps can be taken to ensure you respond appropriatley at such times.

Say sorry If we allow it, our ego will get in the way of what is right, and the simple words 'I'm sorry' are too hard to utter: to do so means that we have to acknowledge that we were wrong. For some reason, we place greater value on *being* right than *doing* right. If we have to *be* right, we will never apologise for our failings. We will always seek to shift the blame. We will inevitably lie or conceal the truth. The simple words 'I'm sorry' are incredibly powerful, but only if offered with complete sincerity and a total openness to vulnerability.

Get rid of the 'but' The word 'but' has all sorts of connotations. The moment we add this small, seemingly insignificant word to our apology we start to shift, or abdicate, responsibility for the problem. An apology isn't sincere if we aren't willing to make a full and frank apology and accept total responsibility; 'but' starts to shift the blame. As leaders, we have accepted a greater level of responsibility. We shouldn't be leaders unless we accept all that goes with the role. This will mean accepting responsibility for a company's mistake, even if you weren't directly involved. An unknown assailant swapped paracetamol capsules for cyanide. It wasn't the fault of the CEO of Johnson & Johnson, but trust in the company was fully restored, and perhaps even grew, because the CEO accepted responsibility and led the response.

Get some perspective When we have made a serious mistake we can easily catastrophise the situation and believe that if anyone finds out, our world as we know it will end. In almost every case this will not happen; things might change dramatically but our world won't end. What is more important: to keep our world intact, or to be remembered for our integrity? It is often helpful to get some perspective on the situation, and if you can't do this yourself, consider asking a trusted mentor who isn't directly involved in the issue to advise you. We get perspective and issues come into focus when we ask for another person's point of view. Things are rarely as bad as we think. What is the worst that will happen when people find out about the mistake? What is actually at risk? List the possible consequences of admitting the mistake and what it will take to fix it, then compare this to the consequences of doing nothing. Remember, just as in the case of the Johnson & Johnson Tylenol crisis, people are always more important than profit or reputation.

Have courage Mistakes have ramifications and the degree of the ramifications will dictate the degree of stress we will suffer. To have courage is easier said than done. We tend to have a false view of ourselves and the amount of courage we think we have; it isn't until we are placed in a highly stressful situation that we really know how we will react. The fight or flight instinct is incredibly powerful when we are threatened and can easily override any sense of duty; all we will want to do is run away, hide, or cover up our errors. Even in the simplest of situations our moral fortitude will leave us, particularly when there is a risk of damage to personal relationships.

The amount of courage needed to admit your mistake directly correlates with the consequences. To draw from that well of courage, you may have to stop – perhaps even remove yourself if time permits – and reflect. It is never wise to respond or commit to action when you are angry or highly emotional. Taking a deep breath helps bring perspective and stops you from succumbing to reflex reactions that will undoubtedly be about self-preservation rather than about what is right.

Consider the consequences When a situation has litigious implications, lawyers engaged to support the organisation will often focus on minimising risk and damage for their clients and their advice will reflect that. At some point you may even need to ignore legal advice and do what is right, no matter what the cost. For years the lawyers acting on behalf of the school advised never to admit the mistakes of the past lest it cost the school more in damages. What may have been saved financially was lost in trust and caused years of compounded damage to those affected. The victims' healing and restoration of trust could only begin with a full and frank admission of guilt coupled with convincing expressions of shame and remorse.

Doing what is right may even involve breaking the law. This was certainly the case for hundreds, if not thousands of people who hid Jews from the SS during World War II; at the time it was illegal in Germany for a citizen to harbour a Jew. Many lost their lives for trying to save another from the concentration camps. In a more recent case, whistleblower Richard Boyle, who spoke out against the Australian Taxation Office's mistreatment of taxpayers, faced more than 160 years in prison for possibly breaching laws on handling public documents and recording phone calls. At the time of writing his case hung in the balance, but what his action did do was to call into question the adequacy of whistleblower protection laws.

In every challenging situation, be encouraged. While at the time it will seem that all is lost and there is no way out, doing the right thing is a true testament to your character and will strengthen trust. This is one characteristic of good leadership that people will admire above all else, and will stand the test of time.

Fix the problem Saying, 'I'm sorry' is the first and most important step when you have made a mistake. However, just to say sorry isn't enough. Highly trusted leaders don't stop at an acknowledgement of their mistake, they go on to rectify the problem. This takes just as much, perhaps even more humility, than an apology because it may mean undoing or changing a decision we have already put in place. Our ego will again be under attack; we will have to continue to be vulnerable until the problem is fixed.

Forgive yourself As leaders, we have the false belief that we have to be right all the time, and that we have to have all the answers. This isn't true. Leadership isn't about being the most experienced person in the room, or the most intelligent; it is about inspiring others to achieve the vision. Alexander the Great was only 22 years of age when he inspired his army to conquer the Persian Empire.

Leaders are human. Humans will make mistakes. While it takes great humility and courage to face up to our errors, we do have to forgive ourselves for making mistakes. We can't let an error undermine our sense of self or leave us thinking that we are unworthy of the continued responsibility of leadership. Every great leader has made mistakes, and some that have cost thousands of lives. While they have accepted the responsibility for those mistakes, and fixed the problems, they have also forgiven themselves and shown up for the job the next day.

Use the experience to grow Some of the greatest learning opportunities come from failure. When issues are resolved, spend time afterwards debriefing, either by yourself or with a mentor. How did the mistake happen? If you had your time again, what would you do differently? What professional development do you need to be better prepared in future? Have the humility to ask for feedback and the grace to accept it.

It is often said that it isn't until you have scar tissue on your back that you become a true leader. Some of that scar tissue is created by the mistakes we make. The healing occurs when we fix the mistake, forgive ourselves, and grow into better leaders through the experience. Only in facing our failures and challenging ourselves do we grow and become better leaders.

#3. OFFERING TRUST

'A leader is best when people barely know he exists, when his work is done, his aim fulfilled, they will say: we did it ourselves.'

— Lao Tzu

I trained to be a primary teacher in the 1980s. I began my career in the non-government sector at a small but elite private preparatory school in the Southern Highlands of New South Wales. School assembly would be held each week. My class was good at lining up and quietly seating themselves in the hall. I was proud that I had mastered the art of organising and moving a group of five- and six-year-old children reasonably quietly and effortlessly around the school to where they needed to be.

But no sooner would my class take their seats than my supervisor would come over and start barking instructions at the children: 'Sit quietly! Thomas, stop fidgeting! Eyes to the front everyone!' Her actions would frustrate me immensely. I had done my job, but for some reason she always felt the need to 'reinforce' my work. Perhaps she felt that I hadn't done a particularly good job, although I never received this feedback. Perhaps she felt a need to assert herself and show the staff who was actually in control, that her job was important. Whatever the reason, her actions left me feeling not just frustrated, but inferior, inexperienced, and wondering whether perhaps I wasn't doing my job correctly.

One of the most powerful actions for gaining the trust of others is firstly to give it. For leaders, this invariably means taking a risk; offering trust and allowing employees to do their job can be hard for managers who believe that 'if you want a job done well, it's best to do it yourself'. This may be so, but does this result in the growth of others, or in you burning out because of overwork?

Leadership takes place wherever people come together in a relationship for a particular purpose. Parents act as leaders as they support their children to become independent individuals. Offering trust in a parenting context can be just as difficult and frustrating as it is in the workplace, if not more so. When my son Alex was a teenager, his Thursday job was to take out the bins. Garbage collection was early Friday morning. Every Thursday the routine was the same, deteriorating into the same tense, angry outcome. Eight o'clock came. The bins weren't out. My wife, frustrated that Alex hadn't done the job would drag the bins to the top of the drive. I would receive an abrupt word because I hadn't been a good father and made him do his job. Alex would sit in his room defending himself, 'I was getting to it.' Everyone is different, and as a result will probably not attend to tasks in the same way you do. No-one enjoys being micro-managed. Your job as a leader is not to create a 'mini-me' but to empower others, enabling them to flourish and contribute their own unique dispositions, gifts and capabilities to their work.

Offering trust doesn't mean that there isn't accountability

or support for growth; it means allowing others to do the job they are employed to do and, if necessary, allowing them to experience failure. All highly trusted leaders who participated in my research saw a key responsibility of their role as being the empowerment of their employees through the offering of trust. Consequently, employees expressed being appreciated and treated like colleagues and professionals, knowing that their team leader was supporting them.

> 'She trusts me, and that is huge. I'm allowed to make the decisions in terms of the day-to-day running of my department. The measure of trust she has in me is allowing me to get on with the job but still providing the support and guidance I might need.'

> 'From the start he trusts you. The behaviour that he exhibits to the staff says, "I trust you to do your best, when you make mistakes I trust you to remedy them to the best of your ability."'

> 'From the very beginning I felt she trusted me more than I trusted in myself. She believed in me. Her recognition … made me believe in myself.'

The role of a leader is not to interfere with an employee's work but to provide feedback or mentoring support if required. The offering of trust means employees are empowered to make decisions in terms of the day-to-day running of their area. They are even empowered to make mistakes. However, the benefits of offering trust go beyond the empowerment of people to perform their roles: it encourages employees to extend themselves and grow professionally, and it has significant health benefits for the leader.

WHEN IT ISN'T WORKING

No-one enjoys being micro-managed: a supervisor constantly looking over your shoulder, barking instructions and providing only corrective feedback can make work life difficult. For the most part people love to learn, they love growing and getting better in their roles, but in order to flourish they need space. Not offering a person the trust to perform their critical tasks, or to make the occasional mistake without fear of retribution, is debilitating. Any sense of enjoyment someone might have gained from their work is taken away unless they feel empowered and trusted.

> *'I feel trusted by my boss. It isn't "you will do as I say because I am saying it". It's a two-way street, you can't have it one way. I have been in the situation where the boss hasn't trusted anyone to do anything and it's just so demoralising.'*

Leaders who have difficulty offering trust tend to adopt autocratic management styles. Their understanding of leadership necessitates compliance from colleagues. Results are achieved through command and control measures: 'Do as I say.' Power is more important to this person than leadership; they have an unrealistic view that they are indispensable, that they are better than anyone else. In organisations lacking trust you might see systems that seek to control employees through manipulation or coercion. This can include specific expectations around accountability measures, key performance indicators (KPIs), performance bonuses, or consequences for not meeting targets. Organisations that don't trust their staff often see the creation of factions, who invariably compete against each other for performance bonuses. They might also see lower levels of staff retention.

I have often wondered about the concept of a staff performance bonus system and what this says about trust. Many people are motivated by money, but this is ultimately an extrinsic reward. Daniel Pink in his book *Drive: The Surprising Truth About What Motivates Us* argues that human motivation is largely intrinsic, and comes from a feeling of pleasure or satisfaction in having done a job well. This form of motivation can be divided into three areas: *Autonomy*, the permission to do a job, to be self-directed (that is, to be trusted); *mastery*, the urge to improve skills; and *purpose*, the desire to do something that has meaning and is important.

Pink says that businesses that focus only on profits without valuing purpose will end up with poor customer service and unhappy employees. Studies done at Massachusetts Institute of Technology (MIT) in the United States showed that higher pay and bonuses resulted in better performance only if a task consisted of basic mechanical processes. The reality is that robotics and artificial intelligence will be replacing these tasks in the not-too-distant future, if they haven't already, so the value of performance bonuses will diminish even further.

As the CEO of St Paul's School I had a performance bonus built into my first contract. These included targets for raising money from the past student community, Year 12 academic results, new enrolments and a reduction in staff turnover. After a year, I asked the Board to remove the bonus. As I came to understand the organisation, its needs, and what its future should be, I felt that the KPIs given to me would distract me from the most important work that needed to be achieved.

I wanted to be trusted to focus my efforts on that work and not some arbitrary targets. To me, taking money from a past student community for the sake of additional dollars in my pocket was not only unrealistic, but totally immoral as I began to understand the history of the school. Nor could I stem the loss of staff when I knew the organisation was overstaffed because people had not been trusted to do their jobs and so had never been motivated by mastery or purpose. Significant restructures needed to occur to realign the organisation with its central purpose and its strategic vision. But the most important work I needed to focus on was the culture of the organisation and the rebuilding of trust. The KPIs I was working to were in conflict with my values and my understanding of what actually needed to occur to transform the organisation.

Like many CEOs, I am often away from the office. On occasions I will put an out-of-office reply on my inbox:

> I will be away from next Wednesday until the following Monday but will be on email and can be contacted by phone. In my absence, Steven will be Acting Head.

After I posted that reply I began to ponder on the message it gave. Does it say, 'I am here to serve, even when I am away'? Or does it say, 'I'm indispensable and you will need me, even if I'm not in the building'? What level of trust am I putting in Steven? Even subtle actions, done with good intent, can speak of distrust.

I know that I am not the only one who is prone to these behaviours. In my work I often travel to leadership conferences around the world. I find it fascinating watching how many executives pull out their mobile phones during breaks. Everyone is checking in at work. 'Everything okay? How are you going on that project?' I know, because I too was a culprit, and would often use this strategy to convince myself I was important, and that people were relying on me.

What happened in the days before mobile technology when the boss went away to a conference or on holidays? They couldn't be contacted. They had to trust the troops to keep things running. My (our) ability to be in touch at all times, reaffirms that *I'm in control*. If I'm not in charge then I worry that I'm not needed, I'm dispensable. So, to continue to be needed, to have an identity of importance, I need to seek to remain in control.

Perhaps you have given similar messages to those you manage: 'When you have written your reports send them to me for checking.' Or, 'Let me know how you get on with that client.' Our ability to offer trust is caught up in our own perception of who we are. If we lack self-confidence we may need to constantly demonstrate our importance, believing that people need us, that we are in charge, and that 'no-one can do it as well as I can'.

If I were truly willing to offer trust, the out-of-office reply on my email should have said:

I will be away from next Wednesday until the following Monday. Steven is in charge.

If we are truly confident in ourselves and comfortable with our leadership capabilities then we would offer trust to others, allowing them to blossom in the opportunities our willingness to be humble provides. You don't have to lead all the time.

WHEN IT IS WORKING

There is an almost universal groan, particularly on the subject of politics, about the dearth of leadership. Whether or not there is truly no-one who could compare with leaders gone by is questionable, but perhaps one of the reasons for the absence of a new generation of leaders is the lack of succession planning. One of the primary roles of a leader is to create a pathway for the next generation. The CEO has made it to the top. They are in charge and have the authority, they don't need to constantly remind people of this by asserting their control. One of their key tasks is to train people to take their place. Offering trust is at its best when the leader delegates effectively, and distributes leadership opportunities across the team, encouraging others to learn and grow. This doesn't mean delegating to the wrong person, or in doing so, abdicating total responsibility. Ultimately, it is the leader who is responsible. In offering trust, their role is not to disappear from the situation, but to stand to the side, ready to provide coaching or feedback if needed.

At its best, offering trust, just as in the practice of admitting your mistakes, requires humility. Leaders who trust others accept that their way of doing things isn't necessarily the only way, or the best way. Great leaders employ people who are better than they are, or allow people to grow to be better than they ever were, much in the same way a parent wants their child to have better opportunities than they did.

People enjoy managing their own work. They blossom when they are given the room to achieve tasks their way. Innovation often flourishes in these circumstances because, as people are given the freedom to do their job, new ways of working or new problems that require a new system or product, are identified.

The idea of a 15 per cent Dream Time, first introduced by 3M company in 1948, spawned many innovations including Post-it notes, and the concept has since spread to other companies keen to keep pace with rapidly changing landscapes. Such an initiative is a concrete example of trust at its best. Companies who have adopted this approach allow their employees time off their normal role to work on a project of their choosing. Apple followed Google's 20 per cent Tinker Time with its Blue Sky program and LinkedIn developed Incubator, which gives its engineers the option of taking between 30 and 90 days off from their regular work to develop their own products for the company.

For these organisations, the 20 per cent time is not a fully-fledged program with its own written policy, guidelines and manager. It is an outlet for the companies' brightest and most persistent employees to see an idea through to completion (or failure). By offering trust to their employees LinkedIn have increased their product offerings to include an internal system for reserving meeting rooms and a toolkit for pointing out new features to users as they surf LinkedIn's site. Google's Tinker Time resulted in Gmail, Google News and AdSense, which now produce over 25 per cent of that company's revenue.

When at its best, offering trust to employees doesn't just benefit a company's bottom line. When coupled with another key trust-building Practice #8: *Coaching or Mentoring*, the offering of trust has significant wellbeing benefits for the CEO, which ultimately means that they can do better work. By offering trust and growing others, a leader lowers their chances of burnout, and myriad other stress-related health issues. This happens because offering trust means that the leader will ultimately make themselves superfluous, so when they take leave they actually can have a break. They can give themselves permission to set proper boundaries and not be contactable, unless there is an actual crisis, and even then, they have grown the team to the point where staff can manage the situation without them.

When a leader can effectively make themselves dispensable and completely switch off while they are on leave, they will know they have done their job well. They will have empowered others to become better; they will have distributed the leadership and grown capacity, and in doing so, genuinely offered trust.

REFLECTION

When a major incident occurs, it is right to stop and take stock. Could the incident have been prevented and, if so, how?

It often takes a major crisis to wake organisations up to the reality that the world is fragile and can be up-ended in a moment. Usually, the response to a crisis is to hold an investigation to identify the causes of the incident, and then design mechanisms, policies and practices to minimise the risk of such an event occurring again. However, the downside of a dogged determination to prevent future crises is that the measures put in place can go too far and end up having significant unintended consequences, restricting the offering of trust.

Following the suicide of Nigel Parodi in 2000, and the very public revelation that the counsellor who had abused him had left an untold path of destruction, St Paul's School found itself in crisis. A class action – a galvanised determination on the part of a group of past students and their families to fight for justice, exposed the school to a potential $18 million in compensation and catastrophic reputational damage.

The head in charge of the school at the time could not ignore the crisis and so began the daunting process of hearing the stories of individual victims as they came forward. The challenge they faced was immense. Unanswered questions give rise to lots of theories. How had the counsellor managed to inflict so much abuse for such a long time without being exposed? Surely staff at the time knew what was happening.

Having wrestled with the same situation myself I have no doubt these suspicions played in the mind of my predecessor as they looked for ways to improve operations within the organisation to ensure that the crimes that had been committed never occurred again. New student protection policies were written and employees were trained – these policies were well overdue and up until then, had not kept up with legislation. New procedures were also created. Staff could not meet with students individually but needed to book a meeting room in the central administration building (which had been designed and constructed in response to the abuse, with extensive use of glass to ensure high visibility). There were even procedures established in respect to documentation, specifying who could access student files and who couldn't.

When I arrived at the school in 2008 I was almost immediately confronted with an oddity in the way people acted and behaved. To me, as an uninitiated new member of the staff, even the physical environment was strange. Barriers had been built to block access to certain areas of the school from general staff. New procedures included unwritten rules about which doors staff could enter by, which staircases they could use, and how they were to address those in authority. The CEO's office was located on the upper floor, to the western side of the new administration building, which had colloquially been named,

'The West Wing'. A confidential photocopy room was next to the head's office, and access to the Finance Department was via an electronic key that only a select number of employees were issued.

While all these policies and procedures had been designed with good intent, and were no doubt a compassionate response by the head to ease the pain of the victims, they had created a culture of mistrust by imposing conditions that exerted a greater control over staff. This new cultural norm had become embedded within the organisation's operations and was reinforced by the suspicions and actions of the then leader. In their minds, staff must have known what was happening at the time but had said nothing; staff had failed in their duty of care of the 120 plus students who had suffered, and while it couldn't be proven, it was assumed that staff had either been complicit or were somehow involved. Trust was withdrawn and as a result, staff morale plummeted. Those who could leave, did. Others were forced to leave. New recruits quickly become inculcated with the cultural norms and found themselves behaving in ways they never would have at previous workplaces.

You don't notice trust until it is missing. It was missing at the school when I arrived. The consequences of that absence were many. The Australian colloquial expression, 'Head down, bum up', became part of the natural way of working. Rather than describing the hard work staff were engaged in, it was used to reference the rife individualism and protectionism that people adopted at work. Employees kept to themselves, clocking on and off at the right time, never giving beyond what they were required, never taking unnecessary risks, and deflecting responsibility for anything that didn't appear in their position description for fear of retribution. Collaboration between employees was non-existent. Innovation was a foreign concept, a distant dream snuffed out by the absence of trust. Alarm bells rang for the newly appointed Chairperson of the Board in 2007 when staff turnover went over 30 per cent.

The unintended consequence of the previous head's actions, in trying to ensure that the terrible events that had occurred at the school never happened again, was the withdrawal of trust across the organisation. But I have sympathy for that response. In the months that followed the royal commission's public hearing of the case study, I too was inundated with calls and visits from victims and their families and the stress of hearing their stories had both an emotional and physical impact on me. My heart literally felt like breaking; heart palpitations were constant, as was the pain in my chest.

At one stage I was befriended, if you can call it that, by one particular individual (let's call him Warren) who gained my trust by empathising with me and offering support: at the time, very few people understood my journey, but he appeared to. However, what Warren did was to successfully plant in my mind (unfounded) suspicions about staff. This impacted on one of the most senior staff members and afforded them less freedom to do their job, eventually taking them off a key project. As a result, leadership became lonelier and the burden of responsibility became heavier.

I found this struggle difficult to overcome. In the end I chose to end the relationship I had with Warren, as it was not only unhealthy for me personally, but I finally recognised that he was undermining my ability to be an effective leader and preventing me from offering trust to the people in my employ. It was incorrect to blame staff. The reality is that paedophiles are masters at concealment. They aren't the trench-coated deviants who we learnt about in the 'stranger-danger' movement of the 1970s and '80s, they are people you would least suspect. The staff at the school would have had no idea of what was happening right under their noses. That is why the counsellor got away with it for so long. It was not the fault of other staff members. They could not be held responsible. If I was to be the leader the organisation needed, I had to hang on to my belief that people are inherently good and deserving of my trust until they are proven untrustworthy, not the other way around. The story of conspiracy could not be perpetuated.

Of course, there will always be an element of risk associated with offering trust. We can never be 100 per cent sure that our trust isn't misplaced; but to be human, to enjoy everything that being human means, we have to believe in the goodness of people. Of course, we have to be prudent and reduce risk, but we can't minimise risk if it means denying people their opportunity to flourish and enjoy the fulfilment that relationships bring. The crimes that occurred could be said to be unforgivable, but trust can't truly exist without an element of forgiveness, and along with it, a willingness to offer trust again.

GETTING BETTER

Your life experiences will have an impact on your willingness and ability to offer trust. For some, particularly those who have been betrayed, offering trust is deeply challenging, if not impossible; for others, offering trust comes naturally. The benefits of offering trust are immense, particularly for innovation. Here are some strategies that can help an organisation to create a culture that speaks of trust, and strategies to help leaders offer it.

Assess your management style What is your preferred leadership style? Autocratic or transactional leaders are less likely to willingly offer trust. Most people at the executive level have access to an appraisal process, but if that process doesn't include a leadership assessment tool to identify your preferred style, you should consider asking to have one administered. Most management consultancy firms, such as the Hay Group, will have these assessment tools available. Alternatively, you could ask your supervisor or Board to use a widely available tool like the Multifactor Leadership Questionnaire (MLQ). The MLQ measures a variety of leadership types and is designed as a 360-degree instrument, considering a leader's self-assessment alongside feedback on their skills from supervisors, peers, direct reports and others. A transformational leadership style sees the greatest propensity for trust.

Remove the red tape The demise of trust we have seen in recent decades correlates with an increase in litigation, regulatory compliance audits, risk mitigation, and policy and procedural documents. In many instances these may be a necessary requirement, but such procedures also limit the possibilities for creativity or innovation. Does the red tape in your organisation send the message to your employees that they can't be trusted to carry out particular tasks on their own initiative? Where appropriate, consider removing unnecessary roadblocks to provide your employees with the freedom to manage their own roles.

Review staff development systems and policies As you review your organisation's policies, review the staff performance systems. What are the key values those systems articulate – are they about performance or development? Are they focused on motivating staff with extrinsic or intrinsic rewards? The word 'performance' suggests that there is a standard an employee has to live up to. There is nothing wrong with having high expectations, but if they are enforced with a system of rewards and consequences, it is more likely than not that the program is targeting the wrong motivational driver. On the other hand, the word *development* suggests that your company is interested in the career growth of your employees. If your organisation has a bonus system, consider replacing this with other incentives, such as 20 per cent Tinker Time. As Daniel Pink, MIT and other universities have shown, people are best motivated by autonomy, mastery and purpose; that is, when they are trusted.

Audit your own communication You may think you offer trust, but do all your communications align with that intention? When you speak with staff, do you offer advice or do you encourage them to solve their own problems? What does your out-of-office email or voicemail message say? If they imply that you are indispensable, or that everything needs to pass through you before being approved, then you aren't offering trust.

Resist the urge to interfere The role of a leader is to empower others to be the very best they can be, not to create mini images of themselves. Feedback is an important tool in supporting a person's growth, but not when it is offered as a comparison, or contrast, between an employee and how you would have carried out the task. If the urge to offer advice or instructions is becoming too great, remove yourself from the situation: essentially, don't watch. What is the worst thing that can happen? Minimising risk is important, but failure is a great learning opportunity. A trusting leader focuses energies on coaching and mentoring rather than coercion and control.

Identify a prodigy or two Who will be your replacement? If you haven't identified talent within your organisation, it could be an indicator that you have issues with your own confidence or identity. Insecurity manifests itself in all sorts of mysterious ways; one of those ways is the false perception that no-one would ever be able to do the role as well as you. A good way of beginning to shift the focus from you is to identify potential leadership qualities in others, and then invest in them. The primary role for those who have got to the top is not to stay at the top, but to make sure someone is ready to replace them in the event they can't do their job. Statistically, there has to be people already within your organisation who could step up into your role. If not, then you have real problems with your hiring processes. If there isn't a problem with hiring processes, then the issue probably lies with you. At this point, you should consider getting some help with what could be a deep-seated personal issue that you need to deal with.

Make yourself dispensable Ask yourself what would happen to the business if you suddenly became too ill to work for several months. If the answer to that question does not bear thinking about, then you have been irresponsible; too much of the organisation's future rests on your contribution and that is a significant issue. Great leaders ensure they have a succession plan in place and that the business is sustainable even when they are gone. Part of the purpose of identifying a prodigy or two is to develop people to take on your role in the event you can no longer perform it. Ask yourself what you want your greatest legacy to be – a company that was fantastic while you were at the helm, or one that continued long past your tenure because you built a great foundation?

Take a break The best indication that you have genuinely offered trust is when you have the confidence to turn off your mobile phone the moment you go on leave, or for that matter, to attend a conference. Leave is about taking a proper break and switching off completely. Your spouse and your family will be eternally grateful to have your undivided attention. They look forward to a holiday with you, not with you and the company. If you can't do this then start back at suggestion one and work through the list to find out where you are letting yourself down, and everyone else too.

#4. CONSULTATIVE DECISION-MAKING

'It's not hard to make decisions when you know what your values are.'

— Roy Disney

In the month of May 1940, a leadership crisis unfolded on the banks of the Thames River, the outcome of which ultimately shaped the future of the entire world. Nazi Germany had been advancing across Europe. The conservative government under the leadership of Neville Chamberlain was frozen, unable it appeared, to make the difficult decisions needed in the face of a looming invasion. The opposition party demanded the resignation of the prime minister, claiming that he was too weak to govern. That weakness was highlighted further when Chamberlain agreed to step aside, but the only person who would be accepted by the opposition to take his place was Winston Churchill. The irony of the situation was that King George VI, who had the responsibility of appointing the prime minister, strongly distrusted Churchill because of his involvement in the failed campaigns of World War I, including Gallipoli. One of Churchill's first decisions was to refuse to negotiate a surrender agreement with Germany, believing them to be *untrustworthy*. Within days of his appointment, Lord Halifax and Chamberlain planned to hold a vote of no confidence to remove Churchill from office.

The whole situation was a drama of trust and distrust. At risk was the British army, trapped by the Germans on the beaches of Dunkirk, France. Retreat was no longer possible, and the evacuation of the nearly 350,000 troops seemed impossible. The navy struggled to land their ships without being pounded by enemy fire. Britain couldn't afford to lose its naval fleet, who would form the last line of defence. A decision had to be made.

Ultimately, it is the leader's responsibility to make a decision. Chamberlain was accused of being weak because he stumbled in the crisis and was indecisive. Almost every decision at a senior executive level is challenging and complexities are often known only by those who have access to the entire picture. Invariably, decisions that a CEO has to make are extraordinarily difficult and carry with them risks, but that is why they are paid the most, because they bear the greatest responsibility. The decision facing the prime minister in 1940 carried enormous risk.

One leader who participated in my research into trust and leadership said to me: 'It's not a democracy, you know, I am the one who has to make the decisions.' That is certainly true but trust is gained by the way a leader makes that decision, and nurtured by the decision-making process they use. There are three broad decision-making practices: decisive, collaborative and consultative.

Decisive decisions are those made solely by the leader. This type of decision-making practice should rarely be used as it is the one that engenders the least trust, and rarely results in the best outcome. In Australia, this type of decision has become known as 'the captain's call', an expression made famous by former prime minister Tony Abbott when he singularly decided to bestow an honour on Prince Philip without consulting his Cabinet. Nonetheless, there are the odd occasions when an imperative decision has to be made. When there is simply no time to seek the opinion and wisdom of others: the decision has to be made on the spot.

Where possible, it is wiser to delay making a decision, particularly ones that carry greater risk. Whenever a decision has to be made that will affect the way others will work, or have an impact on their job roles or their lives, it is far better to give people the opportunity to be part of the decision-making process. How many times has a decision been handed down to you when, given the opportunity, you could have pointed out the problems the decision might cause. How many mistakes could have been avoided if those who had to enact the decision were asked: 'How might it work?'

Delaying a decision gives opportunity for a collaborative or a consultative decision-making process, which involves taking feedback on board.

Collaborative decisions are typically consensus decisions. When true collaboration occurs, positions don't matter; everyone has an equal opportunity to participate in the process. People's views and opinions are valued, and they are able to express their opinions without fear of judgement or criticism. The final decision is made by the collective.

Consultative decisions are ones whereby the views of stakeholders are heard but the final responsibility for the decision rests with the leader. A helpful consultative process encourages constructive controversy; that is, a wise leader will consult with people they know will hold different opinions. They encourage a range of views to ensure that they have considered every angle to make the best decision possible.

Feedback from employees who participated in my research into trust and leadership reiterated that it didn't matter to them whether or not a decision went their way; trust was grown as a result of a collaborative or a consultative decision-making process.

'In my dealings with my boss she has considered everything that I have said, and most of the time she has supported my views. But that's not why I trust her. I trust her because of the way that she expresses why she is not going to do something. She has learnt how to slow down when making decisions. She won't let people bully her into making decisions she needs to think about. I trust her decisions because she consults with staff before making them.'

Trust was further enhanced when the leader explained the reasons for the final decision, while acknowledging the contributions of those who had helped them to make that decision; that is, they had *listened* – the first trust-building practice. People are much more inclined to accept decisions handed down to them if they have a good understanding of the motivating factors that led to them; transparency and inclusivity are key. In the words of one of the high-trust leaders who formed part of the research:

'I work very hard to make sure when we make decisions the staff are informed, and even if they don't like the decision, they understand the reason for it.'

Highly trusted leaders use a consultative process for those decisions that will impact others, but they don't procrastinate beyond a reasonable deadline, instead they act. In May 1940, Churchill found himself in his 'darkest hour', retold by the 2017 film of the same name. He had only been given the prime ministership days before. Even his closest allies questioned his insistence to fight on. At any moment, the majority of Britain's troops could be wiped out and the once great empire was at risk of falling under Nazi rule.

In order to gain clarity, Churchill did something he had never done before. He rode on the London Tube to work. On that journey, he consulted with passengers. Civilians, bewildered at seeing their prime minister riding on the Underground without any security detail, unanimously voted to continue the fight. Churchill asked for advice, and knowing that he had the backing of the people of Britain – people who would have to be called upon to make a sacrifice for the war effort – he entered the House of Commons and delivered his 'We will fight them on the beaches' address, words that will forever be linked to the victory of the Allied Forces during World War II. A daring plan was hatched, code-named Operation Dynamo. On 26 May 1940, a hastily assembled fleet of 800 civilian craft, fishing boats, pleasure craft, yachts and lifeboats left the shores of Britain. In all, 338,226 soldiers were successfully brought home. The impossible had occurred; the operation became known as the Miracle of Dunkirk.

WHEN IT ISN'T WORKING

Decision-making at its poorest can take many forms, but broadly, there are two ends of a continuum of poor decision-makers: the impulsives and the procrastinators. Impulsive leaders default to a decisive decision-making practice, relying on their own experience and wisdom to make decisions. These leaders are either too insecure to ask for help, or have an inflated opinion of themselves, falsely believing that because they are the CEO they need to have all the answers. Leadership in their view is all about them; it is about power and control. The failure to recognise the strength and wisdom of others will ultimately be the undoing of the impulsive decision-maker. To save themselves from their eventual demise, they need to default to an authoritarian mode of leadership, applying consequences for employee insubordination.

If left unchecked, an indecisive dictatorship will create a culture of distrust and fear. Fear is a very powerful motivator, which can lead to cultural norms, such as dishonesty, selfishness, scheming, incongruence and backstabbing. If this does happen, the damage won't be irreparable, but it will take a very long time to turn the culture around and re-establish trust. The journey to repair trust usually begins only with the removal of the incumbent. Even if the incoming CEO practises trustworthy leadership, it can still take a long time for people to recalibrate and feel safe again, particularly if they were the recipients of an impulsive leader's poor decision-making or of a performance management gone wrong. In some cases, such as in my experience, it can take up to a decade for trust to be fully restored. While I made every concerted effort, I had to be patient as people continually tested my motives, seeking to feel safe and valued.

At the other end of the poor decision-making continuum is the procrastinator. These leaders will vacillate between all three decision-making practices, and will either delay making a decision, or put it off indefinitely. Chamberlain vacillated. At a time when Britain needed a strong leader, he failed to accept responsibility for the risks. Everyone knew that there would be consequences for surrender and for a decision to fight on. What they most needed was direction.

My experience with leaders who procrastinate is that there is something in their past that has created a fear of not making the *right* decision. They can make small decisions, but when a complex situation comes along, or one that carries high risk, they become frozen like a 'deer in the headlights', unable to find clarity or a way to move forward. They then run to their closest colleagues looking for an answer, without realising that advice also carries risks.

We are all shaped by our own life experiences. At some time in the procrastinator's story there would have been an experience of a decision they made that didn't turn out well, or they may have been disempowered by a dominant parent figure. They might not even be able to recall the event or experiences, but the impact of that situation has created subconscious protective measures that result in an inability to make a decision when it is most needed. Procrastination has a negative impact on staff, not only stifling their ability to carry out their work but causing feelings of resentment and anxiety. In the words of some of the participants in my research:

'I hear about colleagues in other organisations where they are left for years, wondering if they can even put in a new piece of software to help them do their job better. It is so discouraging.'

'I have been in organisations with a leader who either can't make a decision or sweeps things under the carpet. It leaves you feeling like you are in a "no-man's land", wondering what to do and what will happen next.'

WHEN IT IS WORKING

Good decision-makers are not so concerned with making the *right* decision as they are with making the *best* decision. Perhaps this was Chamberlain's issue; he desperately wanted to make the right decision, but with so much at risk he was paralysed by the enormity of the crisis. Churchill's verdict couldn't be said to be the perfectly right decision: fighting on led to millions of deaths. No-one will ever know what the outcome really would have been if he chose to negotiate conditions for surrender. However, with all the available information and opinion, Churchill made the best decision when it was needed. For his tremendous courage, he won the trust of the people.

Highly trusted leaders default to a consultative decision-making approach. This doesn't mean that they don't use either of the other two approaches; it simply means that their consistent practice is to gather all the available information and opinions to support them in making the best possible decision when it is needed. At its best, a highly trusted leader will identify the decision that needs to be made, develop a strategy for consultation, set a deadline for making the decision, and communicate the entire process to all stakeholders. Having a plan and communicating the process helps allay any fears people may have and will help the ensuing change-management process.

Proper consultation is an open, accountable and transparent process where key issues and concerns are communicated and addressed. It begins with the acknowledgement that leadership isn't all about the power of one person, but is about the collective: all those who will be impacted by the decision. At their best, highly trusted leaders display great humility when it comes to making decisions, demonstrating that they don't know everything; they can't think of every angle or possibility; and that they value the opinion of each individual employee who will be affected by the outcome regardless of their position in the organisation. Consultation impacts on a decision through influence rather than through power; it is about having genuine input into decision-making, not just joint decision-making. To this end, everyone is equal in a consultative process.

To make the best decision, a highly trusted leader recognises their own deficiencies and weaknesses and ensures that they collect a broad range of opinions and views to counter those shortcomings. They don't look for people to support their view; they invite constructive controversy to help them identify alternatives, including addressing the risks and various problems that arise during the change-management process. The opinions of naysayers are highly regarded in a proper consultative process. Often, our natural instinct is to cast aside the view of these people, to judge them as unsupportive, but their perspectives are often the most valuable as they offer a contrasting view.

For particularly difficult decisions, or ones that a leader hasn't faced before, they may seek the advice of a trusted mentor from outside the organisation. A wise CEO will also seek input or an opinion from the chair of the Board or governing body. At the very least, they will advise relevant stakeholders of the problem, the process and the deadline for the decision. It is far better to forewarn all invested parties rather than have to explain your actions if something goes wrong.

When the time comes, the highly trusted leader, rather than placing confidence in their own ability, can place it in the collective wisdom of a robust process; armed with all the information and varying opinions before taking action. It still may take courage, particularly if the risks are high, but they can stand firm in the knowledge that they have drawn people together, providing them with the opportunity to own the outcome.

Once a decision has been made, a highly trusted leader communicates the decision. Their communication always reiterates the problem and the process undertaken, as well as the decision that has been made. Even though a decision might not have gone a particular person's way, communicating the outcome shows how much the leader values the employees' and stakeholders' opinions and views. My own research into trust and leadership showed that for a majority of people the opportunity to participate and contribute to a decision was the act that engendered trust, not the outcome itself. If employees feel valued in the process and understand the reasoning behind the final decision, they will more readily accept the outcome and the ensuing changes, paving the way for a smoother change–management process.

REFLECTION

My own 'darkest hour' arrived in November 2015 when the hearing for the Royal Commission into Institutional Responses to Child Sexual Abuse started. I had read every piece of evidence and every witness statement that was submitted to the Commissioner. I had spent hours with the lawyers preparing my statement in response to the abuse that had occurred at the school where I now worked. I had determined to attend the hearing every day with the chair of the Board and sit anonymously with those who had suffered. For two weeks I listened to the survivors' stories. I saw their bravery and courage. I cried with them, with their mothers and friends. I heard things I really didn't want to hear. Stories of being drugged, raped, molested, hypnotised.

The first testimony took the survivor an hour and a half to read on the stand, retelling what had happened to him all those years ago. How they had fought church leaders just to be heard. Their anger with the church was real and deserved. Another survivor could barely get the words out. Everyone sat silently, giving them the respect they had long been waiting for. Overwhelmingly, the survivors were ashamed of what had happened to them. They were angry that people had tried to cover it up. They were furious because no-one cared enough to listen, no-one had said sorry and actually meant it.

The painful reality of the decades of suffering hit home when one survivor embraced me. He had sat in that courtroom for the whole nine days for friends who couldn't, who had taken their own lives because they couldn't bear it any longer. It was his burden. Who knows how many lives had been lost? Tears rolled down his face.

That moment hit me the hardest, a revelation that I hadn't considered. How many young men had taken their own lives? What of their voice and their family's grief? Would they ever know why their sons had decided to end it all?

I was determined from that point on to give them a voice, to ensure that they were acknowledged as well. I decided to build a memorial in the school grounds to honour them and to make a perpetual apology. The decision I had to make was, what form should the memorial take? I was mindful that if I made a mistake I could create even more damage. The decision couldn't be about me, but needed to include those people who were seeking a restoration of trust.

I reached out to an artist and gave them a brief for the memorial sculpture. Two creative treatments were proposed and I began a consultation process with victims and their families to choose the best option. Opinions were divided. I shared the designs with Archie. He hated them both.

Disappointed, I listened to his views. He introduced me to his wife, an artist who had experienced abuse herself. She proposed another possibility for the memorial. We took these new ideas to the victims and their families. They loved the design. Together, we constructed a garden in the middle of the school, on a location that held special meaning and happy memories for past students.

I had started making the decision using a consultative approach but this evolved into a collaborative process. The conversations yielded a name for the garden: *The Beginning of Peace.* On a cool evening in March 2017, two years after the royal commission hearing, the garden was finally opened. Central to the design was a small hill, some 20 metres in diameter – the climb to the top was intended to mirror the symbolic journey a victim needs to make to come to a place of healing. At the top of the mound is a circle of stone, broken into three to represent the Holy Trinity. Like a mother's arms, these stones wrap around all who enter, keeping them safe. In the middle of the mound is a deep pool of water. If a person chooses to do so, they can cast a stone into the pool and watch their pain be taken away.

On the opening night, people started to appear out of the darkness to join the powerful dedication. Together we climbed the mound in the centre of the garden and sat on the outer ring of sandstone; 116 candles, one for each of the known victims, cast a warm glow within the inner ring. Two large candles, one dedicated to the victims from the other school involved and one for the victims yet to come forward, flickered in the gentle breeze. The names of twelve former students of St Paul's, who had taken their own lives, were illuminated by the light.

Standing in the circle, Archie declared that his abusers no longer had any hold on him. He was declaring himself free. His powerful words brought tears to the eyes of those present.

The Beginning of Peace delivered on its intended outcome to honour the victims of abuse and provide a perpetual apology. The project was a success, not because of anything I had done, but because of what we had created as a group. The collaborative process was the right one to use. It led to a decision that could be owned by all who participated, and resulted in the creation of a beautiful space, a space that brought peace.

GETTING BETTER

Making decisions isn't always easy, particularly when they carry significant risk. There often isn't just one right answer. If there were, it might be easier. But there are things you can do to help yourself make the best decision and grow trust in your leadership.

Make a deadline Highly trusted leaders aren't impulsive, nor are they procrastinators; they make timely decisions. When faced with a decision, begin by setting a deadline. When does this decision have to be made? If it isn't an emergency, then you can set aside an appropriate amount of time to employ a consultative or collaborative decision-making approach. Once you have set the deadline, work backwards to design a process. Be sure to inform staff of the timeframes and the process so they aren't left feeling like the issue has been 'swept under the carpet' and they're 'left in no-man's land'.

Design a process There will be a huge variety of people in your organisation, from the easy-going 'nothing-will-ever-faze-me' person, to the 'control freak' who cannot cope if they do not know what is happening in the next hour. Very few people like change, but if they have the opportunity to influence a decision, and understand when and how it will be made, it will help allay fears and build trust. Designing and communicating the process for making a decision, particularly significant decisions that will impact upon others, will give everyone confidence.

A typical process for a consultative decision includes the following steps:

STEPS	PROCESS
1	Identify the issue, project or policy about which consultation is to occur
2	Clearly identify the goal of the consultation process
3	Decide on the methods of consultation: How will staff have the opportunity to share their views? Will there be one-on-one consultation opportunities, focus groups, a survey?
4	Ensure that participants are clear about the consultation process, including how the information they give is going to be used, and how the decision is going to be made. It is often helpful to publish a 'project brief' once the consultative process has been designed.
5	Use feedback to evaluate the process
6	Follow the agreed timelines

Figure 4.1

Communicate the process Once the decision-making process has been designed, it is important to communicate with all relevant stakeholders. When your employees know when a decision will be made and how they can contribute, it will help allay any fears and uncertainty among staff, and contribute to building trust. When you do communicate, ensure you make it clear what process is going to be used and therefore, who will be making the final decision.

It's not about pleasing people A CEO's role isn't about pleasing people, nor do you become more trustworthy by pandering to another person's needs or acquiescing to their demands. Leaders make decisions that are for the strategic advancement of the organisation. Trust is gained when people have an opportunity to be part of the decision-making process and are shown that their views and opinions are valued.

Invite constructive controversy The strength of any team is its diversity, and the strength of a leader will be informed by the wisdom and perspectives they can draw upon. Consultative and collaborative decision-making are not just motions a leader should enact to appease others, but should be viewed as an opportunity to tap into a wealth of experience that they don't necessarily possess.

Highly trusted leaders don't look for people to support their position; they invite constructive controversy. Pessimistic employees have a view of the world that an enthusiastic, charismatic leader may not have: they serve as an important reality check. When inviting their feedback, ensure you communicate the boundaries; you need constructive commentary not criticism.

Suspend judgement until the deadline Constructive controversy will elicit views that are contrary to your thinking. If you have created a culture of trust, you will find people who willingly voice their disagreement with you. This is an asset, not an Achilles heel. Employ all the skills of Practice #1: *Listening*. Resist the urge to defend your viewpoint. If you become defensive, people will quickly learn that you aren't really interested in their views and are just going through the motions to placate them. Suspend your judgement until it comes time to make the decision. You might even realise that you were wrong and your team members have saved you from a costly blunder.

Examine what's at risk It's always helpful to identify the risks associated with a decision. Not only the risks to the company but also the personal risks. What is actually at risk for you, the decision-maker? Personal reflection can help you identify any conflicts of interest that you may subconsciously hold, which may influence your thinking and create bias. For example, if you are a people-pleaser, you may have the tendency to listen to one or two voices over others because you don't want to get those people offside, or you want to impress them. This is one of my weaknesses. At risk for me is the withdrawal of support or affirmation that I crave from people I respect. Understanding this means that I need to work harder at inviting constructive controversy and finding different sources to fulfil my personal needs. If the conflict of interest is insurmountable, you may have to delegate the decision to another person.

Don't forget ethics Are there any ethical considerations that need to be thought about during the decision-making process? Decisions shouldn't call you to ignore your values and beliefs.

Just because we can, doesn't mean we should, particularly in the current era where technology has the potential of taking away our humanity. For example, just because we have the ability to create artificial intelligence that will make countless people redundant from employment, should we? If you don't stay true to your core values, then people will see you as hypocritical. If you are struggling with a decision that has ethical implications, declare this upfront and include the consideration in the consultation design. This not only makes people aware of the ethical considerations, it gives them an invitation to comment on, or to critique, your views.

Consult a mentor Even the most experienced leaders should have their own mentor or coach outside of the organisation. These are people you can call upon for advice, but primarily they can help you gain clarity about a decision through coaching. Decisions that carry with them a high degree of risk raise stress levels. Stress manifests itself in all sorts of ways, often affecting the clarity of your thinking. A coach can help you manage your emotional reaction and see the issues more clearly.

Provide affirmation Use the opportunity to demonstrate Practice #5: *Providing Affirmation* by thanking employees and stakeholders for their input during the consultation process. As you do, highlight the value you place on their opinions and the influence they have had on the final outcome, including any successful results. Doing this will encourage them to contribute again when another decision has to be made.

#5. PROVIDING AFFIRMATION

'No-one who achieves success does so without acknowledging the help of others. The wise and confident acknowledge this help with gratitude.'

— Alfred North Whitehead

In our fast-paced culture, marketing and the media constantly drive consumerism by reminding us that there is always just 'a little more' we need to make us happy. Social media platforms are saturated with messages that encourage us to compare ourselves with everyone else, often leaving us with a sense that we are somehow falling short of these unrealistic expectations. Being 'busy' has become a badge of honour and if we don't wear it we are left feeling that we are not as worthy or important as others. As we try to keep up with everyone around us, we become so time-poor that we marginalise what is truly important. It is little wonder that anxiety is on the rise. We forget to be grateful for what we do have and don't take the time to thank and acknowledge others for what they do for us.

I have learnt that leadership is often a thankless task. Very rarely does anyone thank their leader. I don't believe this is intentional, but perhaps symptomatic of people's perceptions of those in leadership roles. By nature, we are all quick to judge, quick to criticise and quick to blame if something goes wrong, but we rarely stop to think of the blessings we all receive each day. If you are a leader, don't get hung up on the fact that you may never be thanked for the hours of work you put in. Your sense of value can be found in the lives you have the privilege of interacting with. Even though you may never be the recipient of gratitude, a key trust-building practice is to provide regular affirmation to your employees for the work that they do.

Humans have an innate desire to be appreciated and valued. Bersin and Associates, an arm of Deloitte who research strategies designed to help leaders drive business performance, found that organisations that excel at employee recognition are 12 times more likely to generate strong business results than those that do not.

Study after study has shown that no-one is immune to the motivating effects of acknowledgement and thanks. In 2013 an article by Mark Goulston in the *Harvard Business Review* referenced research which showed that saying 'thank you' not only resulted in reciprocal generosity, where the acknowledged person is more likely to help the thanker, but also stimulated pro-social behaviour. In other words, saying 'thanks' increases the likelihood of your employees not only helping you, but helping someone else, too. In that same year an employee appreciation survey conducted by Glassdoor, an online recruitment company, found that 81 per cent of people were motivated to work harder when their boss showed appreciation for the work that they did. An American law firm, which subsequently decided to adopt the practice, found that people began to work longer hours for less money and burnout all but disappeared. Providing affirmation not only grows trust but also has positive business outcomes. It is well worth taking the time to acknowledge the people you lead.

There are a number of effective ways of providing affirmation. The internet is awash with inspiring examples of emails sent by CEOs thanking their employees. Take the following example of an email sent by the CEO of American Airlines, Tom Horton, as he prepared to leave his position following a successful merger with US Airways.

Thursday, 5 December 2013

A Message from Tom

Dear American Team:
Two years ago this month, we were at a critical moment in our company's history. We faced huge challenges. The sceptics doubted our ability to see our way through.

How did the people of America respond? You delivered! You proved wrong all those who questioned our future. On Monday, we will complete our merger with US Airways, one of the most important milestones in the 87-year history of this airline. In so doing, we will have completed one of the most successful restructures in airline history, or the history of any industry. This two-year journey – which began under extreme conditions – ends with a win for all stakeholders: our people, customers and owners …

This all happened because of you – because you care deeply about this airline and our customers. Your professionalism, dedication and commitment are an inspiration.

Thanks for all you do!

Tom

Emails such as this one often become viral, shared thousands of times on the internet, but they can also be perceived by employees as empty platitudes, particularly when the next media statement declares the significant bonus the CEO is taking home. In 2018 Persimmon, the United Kingdom's largest housebuilders, asked CEO Jeff Fairburn to leave because of the controversy over his £75 million bonus. Persimmon had been going from strength to strength under Fairburn's leadership, but the Board believed that the distraction around his bonuses was having a negative impact on the company. While employees understand that the CEO deserves a greater level of pay than they do, many feel the median pay of the ASX100 Chief Executives of $A4.5million (in 2019) is a little excessive.

To build trust, the practice of providing affirmation isn't a once-a-year activity done at the staff Christmas party, or one-off emails to the entire company; it should become a daily habit, enshrined into the culture of the organisation. One of the highly trusted leaders who participated in my research into trust and leadership said they have made a habit of seeking different ways to value their employees. As they note:

> 'If you've got good staff, you have got a good organisation … If they [the staff] know that you value the work they do, they're far happier.'

A highly trusted leader will employ a range of appreciation strategies including publicly thanking employees at staff briefings, sending emails or handwritten thank-you notes, leaving a basket of fruit on a desk to sustain a team during a challenging project, or simply speaking to a person privately to affirm them. Acknowledgement is given not only for significant contributions but also for the small things people do to assist. Employees interviewed during my research confirmed that affirmation was very motivating, leading to a strengthening of trust because it left them with the belief that their CEO knew them and the work they did.

> 'She does praise her staff very well. She takes the time to write a personal email back to you, thanking you and making specific comments so that you absolutely feel that she knows who you are as a person, which is something that I find very motivating and makes me trust that she knows me and understands what I do.'

> 'He gives a lot of praise which makes you feel good for the small things you do every day. He will often come and see you individually, but he will often do it publicly. It makes you feel really good.'

To be effective, the affirmation you provide needs to be genuine. It is one thing to say to a whole group, 'You are all doing a fabulous job,' but the reality is that such sweeping statements can be a bit like water off a duck's back for those on the receiving end. People want to be told in an unflashy way, 'Hey, you're doing a good job, I appreciate what you're doing.' At the heart of any acknowledgement should be a clear message that the CEO is aware of what the employee is doing and how that work is having a positive impact. A sense of purpose is a powerful motivator. People want to know that their efforts aren't in vain but are making a difference. Simply saying words to the effect of, 'Thank you for the work you do' can come across as trite, insincere and even patronising if they are offered as vague platitudes. A far more effective way of providing affirmation is to highlight the individual or specific difference a person is making, perhaps to the company, to the team, or to a customer.

Like Practice #3: *Offering Trust,* providing affirmation not only grows trust and improves productivity, it can improve your own sense of wellbeing. Studies, including one completed in 2002 and published in the *Journal of Personality and Social Psychology*, have shown that people who practise affirmation tend to be more agreeable, more open and less neurotic. They are more willing to forgive others and are less narcissistic. Essentially, regularly thanking others improves your demeanour, another of the ten trust-building practices, by having a positive impact on your own sense of worth, identity, optimism and wellbeing. It also supports visibility, by forcing you out of the office and onto the floor of the organisation. In essence, if you work on the practice of providing affirmation, another two of the trust-building practices will be improved at the same time.

WHEN IT ISN'T WORKING

At its worst, this practice looks like ungratefulness, the opposite of gratitude, or, in the example of the narcissistic leader, taking all the credit for success. Leaders who struggle or who don't attend to providing affirmation, leave staff feeling as if they are performing a thankless task. The only motivational driver left to inspire them, if they don't find any intrinsic reward for themselves, are performance-based rewards and bonuses, and even these begin to lose their gloss over time.

According to Paul White, co-author of *The 5 Languages of Appreciation in the Workplace*, aside from narcissism there are several reasons why managers, supervisors and CEOs fail to acknowledge appreciation for their team members or employees. The most common reason is a lack of time. Virtually everyone says they are too busy and don't have the time for 'frivolous platitudes'. Other managers are concerned about starting a trend that they may not be able to sustain, or worry about the practice becoming meaningless or perceived as 'inauthentic'. Yet others avoid praise in case it raises employee expectations about how they will be rewarded for a job they are paid to do in the first place. It's a business relationship after all; why do you need to thank someone for what they are being paid to do? Some supervisors worry about what to say, or how to communicate their thanks in such a way that doesn't inadvertently send the wrong message, particularly in the age of the #MeToo movement. Expressing thanks can be seen to carry a risk as it may be perceived by the receiver as crossing a professional boundary, wandering precariously into the personal. Alternatively, they may have had a poor experience in the past. When they attempted to offer appreciation they either received no response, or a sarcastic comment about their perceived intentions. Interpersonal interactions for many managers may be difficult, so they rationalise that it's safer to just say nothing.

Providing affirmation with the occasional, 'Thanks for what you do' at the end-of-year office function isn't much better when the leader thanks only those employees nearest to them; that is, members of their direct team. This limited expression of gratitude may even do more harm than good, creating an 'us and them' barrier. At its worst it gives the appearance that the boss has particular favourites and has no idea about the work other employees do, or the contribution they make to the company. It also doesn't come across as very sincere when thanks are given by a CEO's assistant, or when the thank you itself is out of proportion with the actual contribution – this can come across as over the top and insincere.

WHEN IT IS WORKING

The gold standard of providing affirmation is an individual thank you. This can take many forms including thanking an individual in person, a small gift, a handwritten note, an email or a public acknowledgement. Some organisations have weekly staff meetings or briefings. These occasions could be used to publicly acknowledge an individual for the work that they have done and the difference they have made. Handwritten notes have significant power; they serve as a touchstone for thoughtfulness. A wise CEO uses this tool regularly to show appreciation. At its best, a handwritten note left on an employee's workstation will not only say thank you, but will articulate why their effort was appreciated. Such tokens are often treasured by staff and remembered for a long time afterwards.

For CEOs of large companies, the idea of handwriting thank-you notes for their employees may seem unrealistic, particularly if the company is spread across multiple sites. However, take encouragement from Douglas Conant, CEO of the Campbell Soup Company, a company that has sold products in over 120 countries. For 10 years prior to his departure from the role in 2011 he wrote between 10 and 20 personal thank-you notes every day, six days a week. That amounts to around 46,800 thank-you notes. Under Conant's leadership Campbell's profits soared alongside employee satisfaction ratings. As Conant told Janice Kaplan in her 2015 book *The Gratitude Diaries*: 'Gratitude is universal and it's the one thing that can pull us together.'

Mark Zuckerberg, founder and CEO of Facebook, likes to give himself a personal challenge each year. Not known for his social skills, his 2013 New Year's resolution was to meet a new person who didn't work for the company every day. Then in

2014, perhaps inspired by Conant's practice, he set the goal of writing one thank-you note each day.

PepsiCo's former CEO Indra Nooyi took the practice of writing personal thankyous one step further by sending notes to the parents of her senior staff. She has sent over 400 letters thanking them for raising such terrific human beings who were making a significant contribution to the company. It all began when she became CEO of PepsiCo in 2006. Not long after her appointment, she travelled to India to visit her mother. She found that her mum was receiving constant messages of congratulations on her daughter's success. 'They'd go to my mum and say, "You did such a good job with your daughter. Compliments to you."' Nooyi saw how proud that made her mother, and herself, and so she decided to replicate that for her senior employees.

REFLECTION

One of the 12 names fixed to the inner circle of the stone sculpture at St Paul's School known as *The Beginning of Peace* is Riley. Riley's story is told through his mother's eyes in a book titled *No Middle Name*. Riley was a student at St Paul's in the 1980s. The book describes the tremendous torment and bullying he received at the hands of fellow students at the school, students who were possibly victims of abuse and knew no other way to express their own personal torment. On the cold wet night of 16 May 1997, two months away from his twenty-sixth birthday, Riley took his own life.

I met Riley's mum some months after the opening of *The Beginning of Peace*. Shortly after the garden's opening, sunflowers had been placed under each of the 12 names.

I later found out that they had been put there by Riley's sister. It wasn't until I received the following letter that I realised who had brought the flowers.

Dear Dr Browning

I was deeply comforted on Thursday when you gave so kindly of your time to show my sister, niece and myself The Beginning of Peace *memorial. This beautiful site really does have a feeling of peace and solitude about it. Although it troubles me that such memorials are necessary at all, I am consoled that my late son is both acknowledged and remembered.*

I wrote my book long before I was able to put together the facts that became apparent to me through the Commission's inquiry into sexual abuse in institutions, but now I am able to place in perspective the pieces of the tragic jigsaw.

Thank you for all that you have done to positively and compassionately address the sorrowful history of the school. Although it has been 20 years since we lost our son, our grief is still palpable today, but in the future my husband and I will take comfort in visiting The Beginning of Peace *memorial.*

Once again, heartfelt thanks to you for all you have done to bring some peace and understanding to those of us who mourn not only the loss of a loved one, but the events that contributed to that loss.

It isn't often that you are thanked as a leader. When you are, particularly with carefully chosen words highlighting the impact of your small contribution, it is deeply touching. This handwritten letter delivered inside a copy of *No Middle Name* sits in the top drawer of my desk at work. From time to time I will pull it out as a reminder that the hard work in establishing *The Beginning of Peace* was all worth it. Reading it evokes powerful memories, reminding me that I matter and that I have made a difference, albeit a small one, to someone's family.

Offering affirmation to the staff at the school is a practice I have to make particular effort to do. To keep me disciplined I will buy several packets of blank cards, write a number of them and leave them on people's desks before they arrive at work. I find nothing more touching than the thoughtfulness of a card left on my desk when I'm not there, so I try and do the same for others. I also make an effort to get out of my office as much as possible during the day. It is important to visit people in their area of work and personally extend thanks for the difference they are making. Public affirmation is important to give, but some staff really don't like the public spotlight; even though a person may be deserving, it is important to consider their feelings.

I value people. No matter their role in the organisation it is important to recognise the contribution they make. From the cleaners who come in at night to the Chair of the Board, everyone plays a role and needs to know that they are on the same team and their effort makes a difference. If the school isn't clean and the grounds don't look appealing, then a prospective enrolment won't go past the front desk when they come to check whether the school is the right place for their young child. The cleaner is just as important as the master teacher.

GETTING BETTER

For people with an optimistic outlook, like the extrovert who enjoys interacting with people, providing affirmation comes naturally; this kind of leader may only need a calendar reminder to prompt them to acknowledge others. However, for the introverted leader, or the person who has a more pessimistic outlook, this can be a much harder practice to master. If this is you, there are things that can help you become better at thanking others for the work that they do.

Practise gratitude One of the reasons we don't think of thanking others is that we don't have a gratitude mindset. We can be so busy trying to keep pace with everyone else, or the deadlines that are looming, that we forget to be thankful for what we do have. We forget to celebrate our achievements. Before we can sincerely acknowledge others, we need to have a positive mindset, one that looks for the good in others and in the world in which we live.

Mindfulness research has shown that by practising gratitude we not only shift our outlook but can reduce our risk of anxiety and depression. This is because gratitude reduces the stress hormone cortisol by as much as 23 per cent. You can start practising gratitude simply by writing a list of five things you are personally grateful for. They can be the most basic of things like the food we eat, the job we have, the relationships we enjoy. Make this a daily habit. If you persist, then within two weeks you will have noticed a change in your attitude and your eyes will be ready to see more things in others that are worthy of acknowledging.

Make a daily habit While you are making a habit of being grateful for your own life, form a habit of thanking two employees each day. You could do this either in person, or via an email or a handwritten note. Before you go home from work ask yourself: Have I done my best to thank someone for the difference they are making? Once you have achieved the goal of thanking two people a day, depending on the size of your organisation, consider increasing that number to three.

Look for the difference Everyone desires a sense of purpose. It is one of the most powerful motivators, and the reward of a sense of purpose is the knowledge that you are making a difference. The best thank you is the one that highlights the difference a person is making, either to the team, the company or a customer. Rather than just creating a habit of saying 'thank you', get to know exactly what each employee's role is in the company. If you understand what their job is you will be in a better position to identify the positive difference their work is having, and tailor your affirmation to highlight their contribution.

Use different strategies Everyone is different and, therefore, appreciates different things. For some, one form of appreciation might be quite meaningless while for another, it is very powerful. Some people like to receive public acknowledgement while others find this confronting and intimidating. I once left a bottle of wine on an employee's desk along with a handwritten note, only to discover many months later that the staff member didn't drink alcohol! I haven't come across anyone who doesn't appreciate a handwritten note, but when you start to receive too many of them they tend to lose their value. Get to know your employees and, as you do, your gestures of affirmation will become more thoughtful.

Make it quality A thank-you note may not last long but a card will sit on an employee's desk, or be pinned to a wall of their workstation, for many months to come. Look out for a good source of quality cards and ensure you always have stock on hand. The habit of thanking two people a day will be easier if you have blank cards on your desk as a reminder of your daily goal, and you will have no excuses not to do it.

Celebrate achievements and failures If one of your company's values is innovation, then don't just thank a person for the positive things they have done, thank them for their failure. For innovation to occur, you need to foster a culture of risk-taking, and for this to happen employees need to know that taking a risk and trying something new won't result in negative consequences. Acknowledging disappointments is a way of showing them that their actions will be seen as a positive learning experience. For example:

> 'Thank you for trialling X. While the idea didn't work it did teach us that ... and as a result we will be able to ... all because of your courage and willingness to help our company advance its agenda.'

#6. VISIBILITY

'*What we yearn for as human beings is to be visible to each other.*'

— Jacqueline Novogratz

In business, brand reputation means everything. Big brands make every effort to ensure that their product is distinguishable from the rest. In recent years, the focus on branding has spread to not-for-profit organisations as well. Schools, particularly non-government schools, are employing marketing staff to lift the profile of their product in a crowded and competitive marketplace. Even churches have begun to realise that they need to be 'attractive' to the current generation and one way of appealing to them is to focus on their brand image. Hillsong has one of the biggest church brands in Australia.

The concept of brand awareness has now gone beyond the company. *CEO Magazine* often runs articles suggesting that corporate leaders need to consider not just the business brand, but their own personal brand. The push to increase a CEO's *visibility* requires a deliberate and strategic marketing campaign. The opening words by guest blogger Lesley Everett on *CEO Magazine*'s website in March 2017 called leaders to: 'Imagine developing your personal brand to a level that makes you so marketable ... that the invites come flooding in for panel appearances and presentations.' This kind of visibility, couched as a necessary marketing strategy to ensure that CEOs are seen more in competitive business environments, is really no more than an appeal to a CEO's ego and does not build trust.

For the majority of employees who participated in my research into compelling leadership, visibility had nothing to do with their leader's brand image, their appearance in the media or their stance on political or social matters. Instead, it was all about the *accessibility* of the CEO. In their 2003 book *Credibility: How Leaders Gain and Lose It, Why People Demand* researchers on leadership James Kouzes and Barry Posner found that inaccessible leaders 'cannot possibly expect to be trusted' on the basis of their title alone.

What I have learnt as a leader, as well as through my research, is that trust is enhanced when you are more visible. It makes sense: trust, like leadership, is relational. It is a socially constructed phenomenon. It is consolidated and grown if you connect to and interact with others. People need to see you 'walking the talk'.

I have never met the current prime minister of Australia, but I have met previous leaders of Parliament. If I was asked if I trusted the prime minister, the only qualities I can fall back on are the political party they are affiliated with, the snippets I hear in the media, and their performance on policy matters. I tend to give people the benefit of the doubt. This doesn't mean that I'm not cautious in what I share; I offer my trust to a reasonable degree and the more I come to know and trust a person – the more I become visible to them – the more I will share of myself and the harder I will work. I don't know the prime minister because he's not personally visible to me; I offer him a degree of trust, but not to the point that I would expend any additional energy to turn a policy agenda promise into a reality.

It would seem I'm not alone in this perception. CSIRO's *Australian National Outlook 2019*, a road map for 2060, stated that the percentage of people who say they trust the government has fallen from 42 per cent in 1993 to just 26 per cent in 2016. The report suggests that 'governments are losing trust because representatives are perceived to over-promise, under-deliver and be unrepresentative [invisible]'. The CSIRO's report identified five core shifts needed for our nation's future prosperity. One of these was a call to shift the nation's culture to 'encourage more engagement, curiosity, collaboration and solutions, [which] should be supported by inclusive civic and political institutions'. The report is emphatic in its call for a rebuilding of respect and trust in the country's political processes and leaders. But this won't occur until there is a shift in the way our elected members practise leadership – when they become more in touch with ordinary people and seek to better understand the situations of their constituents.

My research into practices that engender trust taught me that there is outstanding value in getting out of my office several times a day to see what is happening around the place: to listen to the 'pulse' of the organisation; hear people's stories; celebrate and praise the great things that are happening; and to model the expectations that the organisation espouses. The geography of your organisation can also play a part in how visible you are as the leader.

My office at the first organisation I led was on the ground floor of the main building. One of its doors led directly out onto the main thoroughfare. This placed me in the middle of the school where I had a direct connection to the majority of the school community. The office I currently inhabit is on the second floor. It has a beautiful view over the surrounding hills but there is no direct connection to the day-to-day operations of the organisation. It is so far removed from the real work that is happening – the teaching and learning of students – that it can be tempting to bury myself in administration and meetings and never get out into the school grounds.

The idea of visibility could be likened to an extension of the concept of an 'open-door policy'. Many leaders believe in and promote an open-door approach, meaning that when their office door is open anyone is encouraged to come in and share their thoughts and ideas, or drop by to ask for advice on a specific problem. Another popular saying advertised by many leaders is a 'come to' policy to demonstrate they are accessible. However, when promoted in this way, the CEO's visibility becomes dependent on their diary, often via an executive assistant. If there isn't a strong culture of trust already in the organisation then very few people, if any, will take advantage of the CEO's offer to drop in anytime they pass by his or her open door.

A truly visible CEO intent on building a culture of trust takes the concept of an open-door policy to another level: when their office door is open it often means they are not there; instead, they are out on the floor of the company talking with employees. For a highly trusted leader, the notion of an open-door policy is a 'go to' policy. Rather than waiting for the occasional employee to pluck up the courage to come to them, they go to the people. Being visible is a way for me as the CEO to reinforce to staff that leadership is all about relationships, and relationships cannot be established, nurtured and grown unless you spend time with the people you are called to lead.

Being with a person face-to-face allows both parties to listen to, and hear, the intricacies of each other's communication, including body language, tone of voice and the emotions being expressed. It affords the CEO the opportunity to see the issues first-hand, and to really understand the work employees do. Being truly visible also helps a leader to enact the other trust-building practices, such as Practice #1: *Listening* and Practice #4: *Consultative Decision-making*. It also helps with Prcatice #5: *Providing Affirmation* in a genuine way, because the CEO has seen for themselves the difference an employee is making to the company.

Being visible gives the people who follow you the chance to prod and poke you, to see if you are genuine, that you are the 'real deal'. It gives those people who don't naturally offer trust blindly, like me, the opportunity to see who their leader *is*. Are they someone they want to follow, or is their trust going to be misplaced? It gives people the opportunity to get to know their leader and build rapport. The prime minister can't be visible to me personally, but as a leader, I can be visible to people in the organisation I serve.

I have learnt that walking up to eight kilometres a day through the school grounds to be visible is not a waste of my time, but vitally important to my ability to lead and create a culture that enables people to flourish. For those leaders who work in a large company spread across several sites, you cannot possibly be visible to everyone, but you can ensure that you get out and about, engaging with employees to see first-hand what people are doing.

WHEN IT ISN'T WORKING

Sadly, our modern culture places value on a person's busyness, as if somehow the less busy you are the less important you must be. A leadership role certainly carries with it greater responsibilities, and often a greater workload, which is why the salary for a leadership position is higher. However, if a person doesn't keep their ego in check they can fall into the trap of believing that their leadership role makes them more important than others. When this happens, a leader prioritises other work and activities over their visibility; their appointment diaries are scheduled so people come to them, or they meet clients offsite. Their diary is actually so full that any employee wishing to speak with the CEO knows that it is almost impossible to get time with them, and if they were to drop by, the office door would be closed, or their assistant would be acting like a gate-keeper. The notion of an 'open door' is just wishful thinking; the reality is that they are too busy to ever actually be accessible.

At its poorest, this leader is rarely seen by general staff. Most of their interactions are via a weekly bulletin, email correspondence, the occasional phone call, a scheduled meeting or messages delivered by their assistant. The impression this behaviour gives is that the leader is too busy, or too important, to be interested in the trivial matters of the employee. There is no chance of people getting to know the 'real' person behind the leader, and no opportunity for the leader to connect with, and develop empathy for those they lead. When visibility is poor the management style can be termed as absentee leadership, or laissez-faire leadership.

In 2018 Karen Higginbottom wrote about the perils of an absentee boss in an online edition of *Forbes Magazine*. She claimed that the absent boss can cause a substantial loss in productivity and a higher than average staff turnover, which in turn, results in greater costs. To support her assertions, Higginbottom cited an article published in a June 2015 issue of the *Harvard Business Review* titled 'The Top Complaints from Employees About Their Leaders' by Lou Solomon. In the accompanying survey, 1000 workers in the US said that the impact of an absent leader included: a lack of recognition for their work (Practice #5: *Providing Affirmation*), ambiguity around expectations and directions, and a lack of time spent with subordinates (Practice #6: *Visibility*).

Solomon said: 'If you're the kind of boss who fails to make genuine connections with your direct reports take heed: 91 per cent of employees say communication issues can drag executives down.' Solomon goes on to say that the data from the survey showed, 'the vast majority of leaders are not engaging in crucial moments that could help employees see them as trustworthy'.

Solomon, who is also Adjunct Professor at the McColl School of Business at Queens University, often asks her MBA students this question: 'Who will influence you more and motivate you toward your best, the brilliant and well-published professor who has no time to connect, or the brilliant but less-well published professor who makes a connection with you as a human-being?' Hands down, her students always pick the latter. Connection with another person is a powerful motivator.

WHEN IT IS WORKING

Leadership is all about relationships. It is about valuing every employee and their contribution to the organisation's purpose and vision. At its best, a highly trusted leader spends a significant amount of time liaising with their team. They are regularly seen talking with employees and seeking to understand their roles, listening to their issues, working with them to find a solution, and providing affirmation for the contributions they make, including ideas that did not work out.

A highly trusted leader realises that it is all too easy to become disconnected from the workforce and lose touch with the day-to-day operations of the organisation. They realise that if they are distant they can miss out on valuable information about how the company can improve. They know that their credibility is lost when employees have the perception that their boss has no idea what is going on in the company. At its best, being visible not only builds trust, but helps the leader keep their 'finger on the pulse' and respond to issues before they arise and become larger problems.

To this end, a highly trusted leader makes being visible a priority. They build time into their diary to be on the company floor on a regular basis, if not every day; and if they are responsible for a company that spans several sites they will ensure they spend time at each location. At its best, a highly trusted leader gets a lot of exercise.

Being visible provides a valuable opportunity for the leader to 'walk the talk', to reinforce the company's values and ethos by modelling behaviours that they expect of their team. This leader isn't afraid to get their hands dirty and perform the work of others to demonstrate that titles don't matter, that their role is no less important than someone else's job, that they really want to understand the contribution their employees make. They might get on the tools, run errands, deliver the internal mail or complete a print job to model the type of leadership and teamwork they expect of others in the organisation.

When linked to Practice #9: *Caring*, a highly trusted leader will be visible outside the normal day-to-day function of the business. They may be seen attending the funeral of an employee's relative or visiting an ill staff member in hospital. Highly trusted leaders know that to connect with the people they are leading they need to be physically present as often as possible.

REFLECTION

When I commenced my second headship I was struck by a peculiarity in the way people worked, the way they responded to each other and to me. I certainly noticed there was an air of caution when I approached, and for some, I suspect, also fear. One of the first questions I was asked when I started was whether I wanted to be addressed by the staff as 'Headmaster' or 'Sir'. I told them I wanted to be called by my first name, 'Paul'.

I had always worked on the premise of an open-door policy, but it seemed that no-one dared visit my office. Aside from its remote location, rumours abounded about how people were treated when they visited a previous headmaster's office. Even the physical space was intimidating. Plush furniture, impressive joinery all sent a message of superiority and authority. I wished the office was in a different location but the cost of moving it prohibited that idea.

I spent the first 100 days in my new appointment listening to staff in an attempt to understand why they were so reticent to engage with me or approach me directly. With over 220 employees, I set a goal of meeting three people a day. My assistant wanted to make the appointments for me, but

I decided not to formalise the task and instead, carved out two one-hour blocks each day to simply wander around the organisation and casually drop in on people. I wanted to see where they worked, what they did, what they valued about working for the organisation, and how they saw its future.

Being naturally introverted, I had to work hard at these interactions; the task pushed me out of my natural comfort zone, but I soon learnt what a valuable exercise it was. I learnt much about how things worked and began to understand some of the reasons behind the cultural norms that had been established. I was told about a strange habit of one of my predecessors. He would return from leave a day or two early, unannounced, and sneak around to stand behind workstations listening in to staff conversations. He believed this was a good way of finding out what was really happening. His management style wasn't too dissimilar to that of a head I had worked under when I started my career. He and his wife would go through staff members' desk drawers on weekends to see what they could find. This practice so incensed one staff member that she put a mousetrap in her desk!

The Royal Commission into Institutional Responses to Child Sexual Abuse began five years after I had commenced my role as the CEO. During those years, roughly one victim of abuse would come forward every few months or so. Very few came to the school in person to speak with me; instead, claims would come via a lawyer. My role in the process was to recall their student file and see if their name appeared in the counsellor's appointment diaries (which for some strange reason were still kept by the school – all the other physical evidence was gone).

Each time a claim came in, I was confronted with the horrible history of the organisation, but because I never saw the victim

I was detached from their pain. I judged them without really understanding the impact on them and the organisation.

In the weeks leading up to the royal commission's public hearing, I vacillated with a decision. Should I attend the hearing each day, or should I just go when I was called to provide evidence? My question was answered when I read the victim statements submitted to the Commissioner. These raw, honest accounts horrified me: the abuse they had endured as young boys; the denial by the principal; the years of shame they had tried to anaesthetise with alcohol and drugs; and the relationships they had lost.

That same week, the ABC broadcast a story about abuse in an institution in Melbourne. I sat in the comfort and safety of my lounge room and listened to a victim tell part of his story, how he had craved for years for someone to listen and believe him. How he longed to be acknowledged and offered an apology. I knew immediately that I needed to go to the hearing if I was ever going to help restore trust with an important part of the school's community. I was grateful that the Chairperson of the School Board agreed with my decision and committed to coming with me each day.

Our purpose in going was to be physically present when the victims and their families gave evidence: it was about being visible, showing respect to people who had for so long craved acknowledgement. There was no way our apology would ever be accepted if we weren't present as the ugly truth was laid bare.

Archie didn't attend the hearings. Instead, he watched the live feed of the royal commission as I made my apology to the victims and their families. The Chair of the Board and I had carefully considered the words I would say, words we couldn't have chosen unless we had a deep understanding and empathy for those who had suffered. The legal team advised us to remove references in the apology to God, for fear that it would cause offence. But we had listened to each of the victims as they gave their testimony. We had sat anonymously with them in the gallery and felt their pain. They weren't angry with God, they were angry with the church and the principal of the school of the time. Archie wrote on his blog:

> 'Browning says the school has let the victims down. He calls us survivors. I don't. Some didn't survive, and they must not be forgotten.
>
> He unreservedly apologises for what has occurred – he calls the actions of the two paedophiles crimes, not abuse, which is correct – and promises that it will never happen again, that he ... and those that now run the school will not allow it to happen.
>
> His honesty and sincerity move me to tears.
>
> Mr Browning, I thank you too.
>
> I accept your apology.'

It was a powerful moment. To stand in front of the gallery, streamed live over the internet, and give an apology for something that wasn't personally my fault was both incredibly challenging and remarkably humbling. However, the power was not in the words, but in our presence, the revelation of who we were, those two people who had sat silently in the gallery next to victims and their families every day for two weeks. Being visible was the right thing to do.

GETTING BETTER

Leaders can easily fall into the trap of becoming so busy that they marginalise being visible. Leadership is all about prioritising; true leadership isn't all about you and the work that you do, but about those who follow you. You aren't leading if no-one is following, and no-one will follow you if they don't trust you. If you believe in the power of trust and the difference it can make to your leadership and your organisation's success, then you will make being visible a priority.

Plan your diary Before my research into trust, I spent considerable time out of my office and on the grounds. The downside was that administrative tasks had to wait. I did wonder whether I was wasting my time and whether I could be more productive simply by emailing people or asking them to come and see me. However, my research findings showed that being out of your office and interacting with staff has a significant impact; it stands to reason, it is harder to trust a person if you don't have the opportunity to form a relationship with them.

Planning your diary means blocking out time each day, or at least every second day, to simply wander around the organisation and connect with people. Let your assistant know what you are doing so they don't fill that time with other appointments. Executive assistants are also often privy to what is happening around the company and in people's lives; they may be able to suggest who you should drop in on to give a quiet word of encouragement or when you need to employ Practice #9: *Caring*. It's often incidental conversations with staff that are important. They not only help to build relationships, but also help you identify problems that can be dealt with before they become larger issues. Rather than being a drain on time, being visible can save you time.

Look for ways to model expectations Being visible gives you an opportunity to model the values and expectations you have for the organisation and its employees. Why not roster yourself on to a regular activity or task to demonstrate that no role is any less important? For example, roster yourself on the tools for an hour or two each week, the tea and coffee run, or in the case of a school, yard duty or teaching a class. For those in larger corporate organisations, consider joining the health and safety committee as a member, or another committee that connects you with the day-to-day activity of the majority of the members of the company.

Where is your office? The location of your office can have a significant bearing on your ability to be accessible. If you want to work on the premise of an open-door policy, your office should ideally be in a central location so employees don't need to go out of their way for the incidental drop-in conversation. If you can't be in an accessible location, you will have to make more time to get out and about. As you consider the location of your office, give some thought to the decor. Does your office have a welcoming, relaxed feel about it, or is it designed to give a message of importance and position: is it intimidating?

Spend time with the critics and naysayers You have an indicator that the culture is poor when you hear the words, 'The executive team have no idea what we do.' Getting out and about allows you to take the temperature of the organisation. As you make yourself more visible, practise listening. Invite employees to share their views and ideas. Encourage them to express their frustrations. Seek first to understand by listening to what is really going on in the company. The critics' and naysayers' views, while often negative and demoralising to you as the leader, help bring a balanced perspective to what is really going on, and keep you grounded, humble and authentic.

Get a pedometer While it isn't about getting your steps up, the practice of being visible has an added benefit – it gets you out of the office and exercising. People are spending more time seated than ever before and, according to researchers, it is wreaking havoc on our bodies. According to Dr James Levine of the Mayo Clinic at Arizona State University, the concerns are so alarming that sitting down for long periods is set to become the new 'smoking' and has the potential to kill more people than HIV. In response to these concerns, the standing desk has come into vogue. If you struggle to get out of the office to be visible on a daily basis, why not get a pedometer or an exercise app for your phone? Set a daily steps target as a motivator to be visible.

Show gratitude Being visible not only allows you to practise #1: *Listening*, but also gives you opportunity to practise #5: *Providing Affirmation*. As you spend time on the floor of the company seeing first-hand the difference that employees are making, you have an opportunity to thank them for the work they do. (I hope you are beginning to realise that many of the trust-building practices are interrelated. Practising one allows you to practise others, enabling you to become *more trustworthy*. Remember that trust is a socially constructed phenomenon. It appears when people come together and form relationships.)

#7. DEMEANOUR

'Learn to see – to accustom the eye to calmness, to patience, and to allow things to come up to it; to defer judgment, and to acquire the habit of approaching and grasping an individual case from all sides.'

— Friedrich Nietsche

Staffers at Australia's Parliament House will tell you who are the great politicians to work for, and who to avoid. Most elected members of Parliament have no leadership training or experience. They are left to learn on the job. A backbencher has a small staff, but for those responsible for a portfolio, the office they lead can be reasonably large. At any given bar in Canberra, stories about individual politicians, particularly the newly elected, abound. From ministers snapping at staff, losing their cool at seemingly innocuous things, to throwing books and furniture when they are dissatisfied. With a degree of regularity, the national press carries stories of elected members making unreasonable demands. In August 2018, *The Australian* newspaper reported that Labor backbencher Emma Husar took the decision not to recontest the next federal election amid allegations of 'bizarre events' and conduct that was described by many of her 22 staff as harassment and bullying. In her two years as an MP, Husar's office had a turnover of more than 20 people.

The stories shared over a stiff drink late on any given weeknight would not just be about inexperienced backbenchers, but also includes the prime minister's office. Many will recall reports of the erratic demeanour of Prime Minister Rudd, who is said to have made seemingly impossible demands on staffers, which as a result kept the human resources department busy finding replacement team members.

A person's demeanour plays a significant role in fostering trust. This role mostly centres on the notion of safety. When meeting a person for the first time, it is natural to subconsciously ask yourself: 'Do I feel safe around this person?' When we perceive a threat, part of our brain, known as the amygdala, releases powerful stress hormones triggering a fight or flight response: we feel fear. A physiological reaction occurs when our heart begins to pound in our chest and our palms become sweaty. If we feel threatened in any way, our sympathetic nervous system discharges powerful stress hormones, injecting a surge of adrenaline in readiness to take flight.

While the difficult situations and interactions may not necessitate the need to fight or flee, the released chemicals do impact on how our body responds to stress and, consequently, our predisposition to offer trust. The opposite hormone is oxytocin. This chemical is known as the 'love drug'. When our body releases oxytocin, combined with the two feel-good neurochemicals it releases, serotonin and dopamine, our willingness to offer trust increases markedly. When we perceive a person as friendly, caring or interested, our body may release oxytocin increasing the social connection between ourselves and other people.

US-based company Liquid Trust picked up on the neuroscience behind trust and have bottled oxytocin, selling a month's supply online for $US49.95. Apparently if you use it as a cologne people will flock to you, offering their unconditional trust! I don't think the product can be pumped through a building's air-conditioning system, but it does present scope for a budding entrepreneur to capitalise on a quick-fix solution for culture problems at work.

A leader's demeanour will have a significant impact on the way people react to them. If a leader is unpredictable, erratic, demanding or prone to losing their temper, then the natural reaction of any human coming into their proximity is to feel threatened. As they become uneasy, their body will release stress hormones, giving them an amplified sense of anxiety. Their perception of reality shifts, clouded by a heightened sense of defensiveness. When this occurs, the leader's every behaviour is scrutinised and analysed through the lens of an anticipated attack. An inordinate amount of energy is expended trying to determine whether we should take flight, or stay and fight.

Managers and leaders with unpredictable demeanours often result in staff avoiding them, for fear of how they may react. There is much written about the toxic culture of organisations. Many of us will experience a toxic work culture at some point in our working lives and will know how it makes us feel and how it changes the way we behave and turn up for work. In 2012, a federally funded study revealed significant problems with the Minuteman Missileers, a group of highly trained individuals responsible for manning the nuclear weapons silos across the United States. One of the reasons was the erratic demeanour of the leaders. As one of the Missileers told researchers, 'We don't care if things go properly. We just don't want to get into trouble.'

A leader who is seen as a threat will be avoided. Information will be hidden and mistakes covered up, which ultimately leads not only to poor morale and high staff turnover, but also poor productivity and, in the case of the missileer force, exposure to unthinkable risk.

Leaders who have a high degree of self-control engender much higher levels of trust. Even under significant stress, highly trusted leaders will appear calm and in control. When a critical incident arises, or if a team member has made a terrible blunder, they have mastered the ability to remain friendly, approachable and caring. Importantly, their self-control isn't some kind of calculated strategy to lull a person into a false sense of security, it is a genuine expression of consideration and respect for their team members.

WHEN IT ISN'T WORKING

Many a marriage has come undone because one of the partners is never quite sure whom they are going to encounter when they wake up in the morning or when they arrive home after work. I have often tried to understand the reasons for a person's erratic behaviour, particularly a person in a leadership role.

One school principal I knew of was said to be able to charm the leg off a table but had the reputation of Attila the Hun. It was probably during times of high stress that this principal would snap, demanding staff come to his office and explain why they hadn't performed this or that task to his satisfaction. Using his charm he would entrap them, catching them out in their defence, twisting their words to support his judgement of the situation. His office was known as the 'Death Star' because when an employee was summoned it invariably resulted in their breaking down into tears, or being escorted off the premises with a cardboard box under their arm containing their personal possessions. Whether this principal felt his only option was to employ a harsh, autocratic leadership style, or if it was because of his inexperience in such a demanding role I cannot be certain, but what was evident was the impact on the staff at his school. Like the Minuteman Missileers, no-one wanted to get in trouble and so they hid things, or made sure they steered well clear of him. His personal assistant observed the behaviour at close proximity and recounted:

> *'One minute he would be dressing down a teacher like a parent would berate a young boy who had just stolen a cookie from a jar, the next he would be in floods of tears in his office, seemingly unable to cope with the pressures of the situation.'*

People with a lack of self-control can be unpredictable. On the surface they may appear reasonable and restrained but this façade can be triggered, causing them to explode unexpectedly, and seemingly for no reason. The reasons for this can be many and varied, but are largely caused as a result of our life experiences. I believe that a person's outward behaviour is a window into their past. This realisation came to me when I was coaching a person who was keen to grow his career. Peter was a senior manager who showed considerable promise early in his tenure. From what I observed, I had every hope that he was going to make a great leader, even become a principal one day. However, when he was under stress, or faced with a challenge, he would freeze, unable to commit to a decision or take action. His behaviour wouldn't manifest as anger, but as an exasperating indecisiveness.

Even though Peter took the time to consult, over time his team lost confidence in him to make decisions. One day he would be on an emotional high – excitable, optimistic, strong – the next he would be at an inexplicable low, racing from one person to the next hoping to find someone to make the decision for him. His demeanour, while not threatening, was equally erratic. People lost trust in his ability to lead and found ways to work around him so their work wouldn't be hampered. It wasn't until a few months into coaching Peter that I got an insight into his story. I began to realise that his past was having a significant bearing on his behaviour. Rather than using his experiences to make him stronger, he was allowing his story to control him. As a 15-year-old he had lost a sibling after a tragic car accident, where he was left cradling his older brother in his arms. Instinctively, Peter knew that he needed to administer CPR and stem the bleeding, but he froze. Into adulthood he carried the guilt of not doing anything and letting his brother's life slip away in his arms. Until Peter comes to terms with his past actions and forgives himself, he may never be able to manage his demeanour and win the trust of others, which is essential to any leadership role.

WHEN IT IS WORKING

At 9.30 am on 4 November 2010 flight QF32 left Singapore bound for Sydney. The Airbus A380 carrying 469 passengers and crew had only recently been purchased by Qantas and had only completed a handful of flights. At the command was 55-year-old Richard de Crespigny, a pilot with over 15,000 hours of experience.

As fortune would have it, there were four other pilots on the flight deck that day: Harry Wubben (route check captain), Matt Hicks (first officer), Mark Johnson (second officer) and David Evans (sitting in the observer's seat). As a team they boasted over 140 years of experience.

Just four minutes out of Changi Airport, as the plane climbed through 7000 feet, there was a loud bang, followed by another noise like a car backfiring. The number-two engine exploded. Shards of metal sliced through the wing tearing a hole several feet across. A fuel tank caught fire. Panic broke out in the main cabin. Passenger Marion Carroll could see metal sticking out of the wing. She prayed that the end would be swift. In the cockpit a terrifying cascade of Electronic Centralised Aircraft Monitor (ECAM) failure messages poured in. Each needed to be actioned. The engine needed to be disabled and the remaining three throttled back. The hydraulics, brakes, electrics, fuel, flight control and landing systems were all compromised.

Apart from the audible warnings and messages flashing across almost every control screen, there was absolute calm in the cockpit. De Crespigny and the other pilots with him began to work through 125 checklists, an unprecedented number, considerably more than they had ever trained for in the flight simulator. 'We were in a state of disbelief. We were worried, but our training kicked in,' de Crespigny said later.

Under instruction from the captain, the flight crew set about bringing calm to the passengers. Roughly every 10 minutes they made a public address, updating the passengers on their current situation. The plane was heavily laden and they didn't have the ability to dump the excess fuel. This meant that they were 50 tonnes over their maximum landing weight. To top it off, the crew had no anti-skid brakes and could rely on only one engine for reverse thrust. The co-pilots had to calculate the approach speed and work out if there would be enough runway to bring the crippled plane to a halt in time.

There probably isn't a more stressful situation: a pilot and his team responsible for 469 passengers and crew facing a situation that no-one is fully prepared for. One could easily forgive de Crespigny for losing his cool and barking orders to the crew. But he didn't. He kept calm. It was an extraordinary situation. By rights, with an avalanche of ECAM messages, some contradicting others, the plane should have come down in the ocean. But with ice-cold nerves, de Crespigny and the team defied the odds and continued to fly the plane, landing four hours later back in Singapore with 150 metres of runway to spare, blowing four tyres but saving all on board.

When asked later whether they would have been able to land the plane with the standard crew of two de Crespigny wasn't sure. The passengers on flight QF32 were fortunate that day to have five experienced pilots on the flight deck. De Crespigny never forgot that he was in charge, but the team instantly divided the tasks, working together to trouble-shoot and confirm decisions. The golden rules of Airbus were adhered to – aviate, navigate, and communicate. The traits of Qantas pilots, ingrained through training – disciplined collaboration, readiness to speak up, being thorough and *staying calm* – resulted in what was later described as a miraculous outcome.

REFLECTION

Anger is one thing, fury and rage are quite different. I have experienced a person's fury a number of times: an irrational, frightening, uncontrolled anger. In May 2018 I took a phone call from a past student called John. Something had triggered a memory for him, and that memory had sent him spiralling into a psychosis. He told me how he had been raped as a seven-year-old by a family member, and then in 1992 he had barged into the school counsellor's office to ask for careers advice, only to find the counsellor abusing another student. I could only listen as John yelled uncontrollably down the phone for 30 minutes.

John called again a few days later. The conversation began calmly. I was hopeful that I could share with him a few details that he wasn't aware of that might give him some answers. Unfortunately, John's anger escalated rapidly. He began making all kinds of threats against me and against the school. He was looking forward to waging an online campaign in retaliation. He was going to enjoy getting the justice he so longed for. It was obvious that John wasn't aware of the admission of guilt that had been made during the royal commission hearing, the apology that had been given, or the garden that had been built. He hung up again before I could say anything.

Two weeks later, John called again. The pattern was similar. The conversation began in a reasonable manner. He wanted to know who was ultimately responsible for his welfare when he was a student. But just like the previous calls, John's anger quickly escalated into a rage. It was a draining experience. Each time John called, it left me rattled for days afterwards. While logically I knew that John was not angry with me, my flight or fight instinct told me otherwise. Try as I might to suppress it, as I listened to John it was incredibly difficult not to take a defensive position.

After a few further phone calls, John turned up at the school unannounced during a holiday break. Reception called my office to say he was in the foyer and wanted to meet me. My immediate response was one of fear. I could feel the blood drain from my face. John was unpredictable. He was angry. He was struggling to see past his emotions, and rightly so. I knew he wanted retribution, but what did he want from me: justice?

With trepidation I went downstairs to meet John face-to-face. He was dressed in a suit, not at all the person I had imagined. My eyes instinctively glanced to his pockets. He didn't appear to be carrying anything that could cause me harm. I had my phone in my pocket just in case. He invited me to go outside. I made sure we stopped where others could see us. John reached into his pocket and drew out a case of cigarettes. His hands were shaking. As he took a cigarette to his mouth, he told me that he had only just taken up smoking in the last few weeks. He apologised for his behaviour on the phone, but his anger was still there. You could see it in his eyes. He was controlled for the moment, but you could tell that John was still seeing the world through his pain.

I asked John if I could show him something. He recoiled. His face contorted as if he were about to launch into another tirade. He didn't want to see the counsellor's room where he had witnessed abuse all those years ago. I took him to the garden, *The Beginning of Peace*. There we sat together for two hours as John wept for the boys who had lost their lives. His guilt for not doing more to save them poured out.

I learnt a lesson that day. I realised how willingly and quickly I had judged John without really trying to understand him or why his behaviour was so erratic. My fear had led me to expect the worst. We place people in neat boxes, making decisions about who we will form relationships with, who we will trust and who we will avoid. We gravitate to people we perceive as having an interest in us as a person, or who share similar values and interests, and avoid those we consider a threat. Our irrational self-preservation instincts cause us to be selfish. We would rather conserve the emotional energy it takes to be around a person who appears irrational, erratic and unpredictable, than reach out to bring healing to a fellow human.

As John told me his story and I witnessed the physical distress it caused him, as I sat with him while he wept for the friends he had lost, the anxiety and fear I felt subsided. Every time John had contacted me my natural instincts had told me to hang up the phone when he called, or to respond to his anger and abuse with equally foul language. But having seen the impact of abuse so many times before I knew that John wasn't actually angry with me. While he threatened me many times, I knew he meant no harm, he just wanted someone to listen.

Leaders do have a greater responsibility to manage their emotions, even when we come across people who are struggling with the pain of the past or a frustration in the present. People who choose to follow us have a higher expectation of how we should behave. During a crisis, people want their leaders to provide reassurance. The steely nerves of Captain de Crespigny saved the lives of everyone on board flight QF32 that day. As challenging as our encounters were, John helped me strengthen my ability to 'retrain my mind' to process life as it is.

GETTING BETTER

We are each shaped by our life experiences. These experiences influence the way we behave and respond in certain situations, especially when we are under stress. Some people have a very high tolerance for stress and thrive when things are incredibly challenging, while others crumble and hide. Stress manifests itself in all sorts of ways, including in our demeanour. The first key to leadership is to get to know yourself – who you are, what your triggers are, and how your body reacts to stressful situations. Controlling your demeanour, the outward expression of what you are feeling internally, is an important trust-building practice. Here are some suggestions that could be of benefit:

Face your past Scott Peck opens his book, *The Road Less Travelled*, with the words, 'Life is difficult.' He argues that suffering is a natural part of life, but those who do not have the courage to face their demons and work through them never grow to lead flourishing lives. Trauma is a terrible thing, particularly if experienced during childhood. Many people who have been through a terrible event go on to lead well-adjusted lives while others struggle immensely. If you are someone who experiences emotional highs and lows or is prone to losing your temper inexplicably, then maybe it is an indicator of a deep pain that you have buried and long ignored. If this is you, then perhaps it is time to ask someone to walk the journey to healing with you.

What are your triggers? We all have our own pet hates and annoyances. For me it is inauthentic people, who gush praise on me for their own gain (that's me being judgemental!). They really get up my nose. I need to work hard to be in their company. I am sure that when they walk towards me my facial expression reveals my sentiments. What are your triggers? Understanding what can cause you to become frustrated, annoyed or angry is the first step to learning how to manage your demeanour. Once you identify your triggers, you can develop strategies to help you manage them. I have a few prepared responses to the questions I know those insincere people will ask me. I try to respond with good grace.

Manage your facial expressions We may think we are able to manage our emotions and control what comes out of our mouth, but what we may not realise is that our face can say it all. Our facial expressions are triggered by our conscious and subconscious interpretations of events and situations. These reactions are the visible manifestation of the emotions we are feeling. These reactions happen so quickly that we become aware of them only once we've made them, and then it is too late. Sometimes we aren't aware of the expression on our face at all, even though it has been there for quite some time. While we might think we seem calm, biting our tongues and taking deep breaths, our subconscious reactions may tell another story. Consider asking a trusted colleague or mentor for feedback on your facial expressions and your non-verbal communication. Ask them to pay particular attention to your body language in meetings or during difficult conversations. The more you become aware of how your emotions manifest themselves, the more you will be able to control your demeanour.

Prepare for the worst The pilots on board QF32 had been trained for every possible scenario (though perhaps not to the degree they experienced that day coming out of Singapore). When the number-two engine exploded, they calmly began working through the checklists, bringing the plane back under control and reassuring the passengers and crew. Even though I have been a school principal for more than 20 years, there are still things that I have never come across before. With time we all become more experienced, but a critical event waits for no-one. It is sometimes best to prepare for the worst and then be pleasantly surprised by the reality. Instead of a flash of panic, you will be more controlled if you have a plan to tackle the difficulty.

Vent Even though trust in our leadership demands a high degree of self-control, we are still human. I get upset, hurt, stressed and angry. Bottling up my emotions is not helpful. If you keep those emotions inside, they are going to manifest themselves in other ways. While you may be an expert at controlling your demeanour, it is still important to take care of yourself. A trusted colleague, partner or health professional can provide you the safe space you need to release what you have been trying so hard to contain. Captain de Crespigny spent many hours with a psychologist after the critical incident on flight QF32 to help him work through the impact that event had on him.

#8. COACHING OR MENTORING

"'The real power of effective leadership," writes Brigadier Jim Wallace, former head of Australian Special Forces, "is maximising other people's potential.'"

— John Dickson, *Humilitas*

I was just 31 when I was first appointed as head of an independent school. For the first few years I struggled with my age – a good portion of the staff were older and far more experienced than me. This reality would often leave me feeling intimidated and like I was less worthy. I felt even more inadequate when I attended conferences where other heads boasted about the number of staff they had supported before they went on to become principals. What did I have to offer aspirational staff when I had far less experience and no expertise as a coach or mentor? It took me a long time to accept that I was the appointed leader and that one of my primary roles as leader was to maximise people's potential and grow the next generation of leaders.

There is a difference between coaching and mentoring. Coaching is task-orientated and performance driven, while mentoring is relationship-orientated, development driven and typically long term. Neither role has a greater impact on the development of trust than the other; what is most important to staff is their leader's investment in their development and career growth. Trust in this practice, like most of the other trust-building practices, is the realisation that leadership isn't all about the CEO but about the growth of the rest of the team.

Leaders wear multiple hats. Most are comfortable with managing the performance of their direct reports to fulfil their work agenda. Standard management practices can be as simple as offering suggestions or advice about how to perform a particular task, setting targets, monitoring results, and improving quality and efficiencies. All organisations need good managers, and good leaders should have sound management skills, but occasionally managers and leaders fall into the trap of solving issues themselves and giving direct commands to employees, or worse, employ an autocratic style of leadership to achieve their KPIs. When this happens it can make a leader look like a 'hero', the expert who has been brought in to repair damage and maximise outcomes, and is seen to 'save the day'.

In the current economic climate, more and more Boards are seeking a quick-fix solution to counteract uncertainty and unpredictable change. With the appointment of a new 'hero' leader comes a new strategy. For many companies an appointment of this nature has paid dividends, at least in the short term. But at what expense?

When an organisation's performance is poor, many leaders default to what they believe will yield quick turn-around results. They employ robust management techniques and autocratic leadership practices, instructing people on their preferred way to work because they have experienced success in the past and have been brought in to implement change. However, the hero CEO approach rarely, if ever, results in lasting positive organisational change. Lasting change and more profound positive impact is achieved through the empowerment of others, both in trusting them to do the work and in finding new and innovative solutions.

While most leaders are familiar with management practices they are less clear about how to support a person's development, apart from typical professional learning that includes training courses, conferences and workshops. According to the Center for Creative Leadership's research, most people would like their managers to coach them but say that this doesn't happen enough. And part of the reason for this is that most managers don't have the knowledge of basic coaching techniques that could benefit, enable and help develop their teams to perform more effectively.

As a leader, I am often second-guessing myself. It took me years to understand what it is to coach someone else. Before I did, I felt that I didn't have anything of value to give and I certainly never saw myself as the expert, particularly when a good portion of the staff were more experienced than me. However, coaching behaviours can be as simple as providing feedback to promote growth, or as powerful as challenging a person's thinking. One of the main goals of any coaching session is listening with the intent to help the coachee unlock their hidden potential. Coaching is about asking, while managing is about telling.

Over time I have learnt that to coach someone else does not mean that I need to be the expert. Coaching is not about giving advice or telling people the answers. Coaching is about empowering the coachee to find their inner confidence, help them to grow and come up with their own solutions. Advice is often not as effective because everyone is different and we all bring our own style to the role of leader. If I offer advice to others born out of my own experiences it is possible that my advice won't be as successful; my approach may not suit their style and abilities. Good coaches don't try to create a 'mini-me'.

Coaching can be an informal relationship, where the leader uses a situation to identify possible avenues for development and growth, gives real-time feedback, challenges the person's assumptions, and/or provides affirmation for new behaviours. Alternatively, coaching can be a formal process that entails a series of conversations or collaborative dialogues in which the leader works with the coachee to evaluate a given situation, agree on new behaviours, develop an action plan, and follows up to keep the coachee accountable and provide affirmation.

At the heart of coaching is the ability to ask the right questions. Questions help the coachee to reflect deeply, to cut to the heart of the problem and understand how they are feeling about it. Great questioning should help a coachee identify what is at risk if they do nothing, or if they choose a particular response or strategy. A coach then provokes a coachee to brainstorm solutions, identifying the strengths and weaknesses of each possibility. A coach assists the coachee to recognise their preferred solution and encourages them to take action.

An effective coach rarely, if ever, suggests solutions. They listen carefully. They help the person understand and articulate how they are feeling. They help the person understand themselves better and to see the situation from a different perspective. They also encourage the coachee to find their own inner strength, courage and confidence, and to believe in themselves.

WHEN IT ISN'T WORKING

A person I was once chatting to about trust and leadership shared with me an anecdote about working for a large PR firm. Whenever a member of their team made a mistake the boss would email all staff to highlight the error. This wasn't a one-off, but a regular practice. The CEO used this and other tactics to exert their authority, like pitting the publicists against one another to bring in bigger, higher-paying clients. These strategies worked for a little while – profits lifted – but it created a cutthroat culture where productivity was motivated by fear. Eventually, the CEO's desire to exert control through the use of manipulative practices left the team members feeling resentful, demoralised and fearful of the next encounter. No-one had the opportunity to grow professionally.

Leaders, like the one described above, can have an inflated view of themselves and a false sense of their abilities. Either that, or they have poor self-confidence that has resulted in a paranoia that they might be shown up by someone if they stop the masquerade that they know best. Whatever the reason, coaching or mentoring is at its poorest when it is non-existent, when the leader always falls back on basic management practices or an autocratic style of leadership to achieve their goals, without investing time in their people. The greatest mistake you can make as a leader is believing that you are better than anyone else.

All too often I have seen leaders falling into the trap of thinking that because they are in charge they need to be the font of all knowledge, the wisest person in the organisation, the judge, jury and executioner. Falling into this trap all but ensures a cycle of mistrust. The tragedy of this thinking is that the collective wisdom and experience within the organisation is never capitalised on, and the company is never any better than the person at the top. Sometimes this trait can be identified in the words the person uses: 'My company, my staff, my Board'. We could call it 'arrogance', but as most of us would be appalled by the idea of being called arrogant, let's call it a 'fixed mindset'. According to Carol Dweck, author of *Mindset*, fixed-mindset leaders live in a world where some people are superior and some are inferior. These leaders repeatedly affirm their superiority.

Leaders who have a fixed mindset are doomed to failure at their own hands. They are not able to admit to or correct their mistakes and deficiencies. They're constantly trying to prove that they're better than others. Fixed-mindset leaders don't really want to work with teams, they want to be the only 'big fish' and try to intimidate people with their brilliance. As Dweck notes, most managers and CEOs are not leaders and fail to transform their organisations despite weilding power.

When a leader has a fixed mindset, everything within the organisation revolves around the boss. When this occurs, everyone takes on a fixed mindset by default. Instead of learning, growing and moving forward, everyone starts worrying about being judged – and trust disappears.

WHEN IT IS WORKING

At its best, the practice of coaching or mentoring encapsulates six out of the 10 trust-building practices in action: *Listening, Offering Trust, Demeanour, Providing Affirmation, Caring,* and *Keeping Confidences.* Wise leaders know when to switch from managing, to coaching or mentoring. They have a growth mindset and see others in a positive light, recognising their desire to improve.

Highly trusted leaders know that leadership isn't all about them. They recognise that their company or organisation is only as good as the people working for it, so it is in their best interests to employ people with the potential to be better than they themselves are, and to help them grow. They are content in the knowledge that they are the leader; that, in arriving in that position, a key role is for them to grow the next generation of leaders. Thus, they make coaching or mentoring a priority, regularly creating opportunities to build informal relationships with staff to provide ad-hoc coaching or, having identified people keen to grow, scheduling time in their diary to accommodate a formal coaching session.

If you are the recipient of coaching or mentoring, you will know when it is at its best because your CEO, supervisor or leader:

- has your best interests at heart;
- is focused on you when they meet with you;
- gets to know you well enough to know exactly how to motivate you and help you grow;
- makes you do all the work rather than giving you advice or the answers to your problems;
- provides you with enough support to allow you to succeed;
- allows you to make some mistakes and isn't critical or demeaning when you do;
- provides you with clear expectations so you understand what success looks like and can set achievable goals; and
- is committed to giving you honest feedback.

These feelings are evoked both in formal and informal coaching sessions. You are never left feeling as if you will never meet the standards required; instead, you will be inspired to set goals and to achieve more than you ever thought possible.

In a formal setting, a highly trusted leader will use any number of coaching models to structure their conversation with you, such as the GROW model (see Figure 8.1) for problem solving and setting realistic goals by asking the following questions.

Goals	What would you like to achieve?
Reality	What is the current situation?
Options	What could you do to achieve your goals?
Will	What will do you do?

Figure 8.1

The GROW model is perhaps the most commonly used coaching model. The simple, structured approach focuses the conversation on the coachee, helping them to identify their problem, understand what is holding them back from achieving their goals, and specify the actions they will need to employ to resolve the issue or find solutions.

A more comprehensive coaching model is offered by the Center for Creative Leadership. The RACSR Model (see Figure 8.2) has a focus on building a strong relationship between a coach and coachee and highlights the responsibility of the coach to provide support. This model is more comprehensive with a focus on developing rapport. It suggests that coaching won't be as effective unless there is a foundation relationship in place, built on trust. Only once this relationship is established will a coachee be more willing to receive honest feedback and accept support.

At the relationship-building stage in the RACSR framework, a typical question the coach may ask is: 'What can I do to help you achieve your goals?' An offer of help demonstrates that the leader is truly invested in the development of the coachee.

Relationships	Establish boundaries and build trust
Assessment	Create awareness through feedback, encouraging discovery and insight
Challenge	Challenge thinking and assumptions, promote practice
Support	Listen for understanding, offer support, sustain momentum
Results	Set goals

Figure 8.2

REFLECTION

Knowing that coaching was a weakness in my leadership practice, I committed to doing a training course to learn how to improve. I enrolled in a three-day intensive workshop run by the Center for Creative Leadership. The pre-course work included a Myers Briggs personality assessment and the administration of a 360-degree tool to gather feedback about my current skills and abilities (feedback being part of the *Assessment* stage in the RACSR Model).

The workshop was made up of seven attendees from the corporate sector, mostly international companies from

China, Indonesia, India and the Netherlands. Their stories about pressures to meet key performance indicators (KPIs) by set deadlines were consistent across sectors and regions. The frustration on the part of the managers within these organisations is profound, as they face a continuous internal conflict – on the one hand they have a deep empathy for people, while on the other they are compelled to reach targets or risk their own position. The temptation to default to a command and control style of leadership was often too difficult to resist, particularly when deadlines were tight.

Like me, these managers wanted to learn how to become an effective coach. They genuinely wanted to see their colleagues grow. While each organisational context was different, the issues managers faced were not dissimilar to my own experience in the education sector: under-performance of staff, staff conflict, competing expectations of people, failing teams, demanding superiors and customers. It was also interesting to learn that people's perceptions of trust was the same irrespective of their cultural background.

The coaching workshop taught me several valuable lessons. Primarily it taught me the art of listening. Through feedback, role-play and coaching, I realised that I was judging people and situations far too early. I wasn't following Covey's rule: 'Seek first to understand before being understood.' Instead of suspending my judgement I was reaching a conclusion about situations and people far too early, and then, as I listened further, I was gathering evidence to support my conclusion. This meant that I was ignoring important pieces of information they were trying to communicate and, as a result, I was often wrong in my assessment. I couldn't help people realise their potential if I didn't properly understand them, or their situation.

While I was attending the workshop, I received a phone call from my office. The Risk and Compliance Officer was worried about a past student who had called the school looking for me and had started making all manner of threats. They were worried that on my return I would be in danger.

I had met the former student in question, Trevor, on a number of occasions. He had called me several times to vent, the anger he was experiencing was not dissimilar to that of other victims, but with one exception. Trevor claimed that he hadn't been sexually abused.

Trevor has scoliosis, or a curvature of the spine, which was quite pronounced. He told me that, because the other school children perceived him as different, he had been picked on incessantly at the school when he was a boy. The bullying was so severe that he would often escape the grounds, only to be punished for his truancy with 'six of the best' across his palm. He told me that he once went to see the counsellor: 'He tried it on with me, but I threw a table at him and bolted straight out of there. I got the cuts for that too.'

The bullying he experienced was unrelenting, cruel and often sadistic. There was no respite. The impact on him as a victim meant that now he was living on and off the streets. He had issues with drugs and had spent time in prison. His family had long given up on him. They never really understood or knew what had happened.

At one stage, Trevor told me he was diagnosed with Berserk Syndrome. He claimed that his destructive behaviour and tendency for violence was beyond normal anger. Whether that was true or not, his paranoia was palpable. During one call to me he was convinced the police were circling his house in a helicopter, and the Tactical Response Team was about to bust the door down at any moment to confiscate his collection of machetes and medieval weapons.

My initial reaction when the Risk and Compliance Officer rang was one of panic. However, the words *suspend judgement* were in my head. I had spent time with Trevor. We had developed a relationship of trust. He would freely share his feelings with me, and as a result I had learnt to understand how life had shaped him into the person he is today. The violent threats were bravado, a façade, a learnt behaviour to protect himself from the playground bullies. The collection of medieval weapons was real enough, but he meant me no harm.

When I returned from the course I decided to try a coaching approach with Trevor, with the goal of helping him take back control of his life. I had already built a rapport of trust with Trevor and he knew I was a person who wanted to help. In our following meetings I continually reminded myself to simply listen and not judge. I asked clarifying questions to help him understand himself better. We discussed his options for dealing with his issues and seeking compensation, and I offered to support him in his decisions as best as I could. While I didn't want to (because it was such a draining experience) I followed up with Trevor several times over the following months to find out how he was going with his preferred course of action.

In supporting the past student community (and for that matter, current staff who on occasion also experience challenges) I sometimes need to be a counsellor. Adopting a coaching style is a powerful way of supporting those in need: build a relationship of trust, understand the problem (postponing judgement), challenge the thinking (is there really a police helicopter?), offer support and set goals. In my case, the relationship was about empowering victims to take back control of their lives and, in many cases, agree to seek appropriate professional counselling.

Trevor, like so many others I have met, taught me more about myself and helped me appreciate that we are all people of value. We can learn profound things from the most unexpected sources. I've taken the lessons I learnt from that course, and the experiences I have had with past students like Trevor into the workplace to strengthen my resolve to support the growth of others.

GETTING BETTER

Formal coaching is all about asking powerful questions to assist others in finding their own solutions. Using a structured approach is a helpful way of moving the coachee along a journey of reflection and self-discovery to a point of setting goals and taking action. Listening is central to coaching. When the person you are coaching shares their story remember that communication is 55 per cent body language, 35 per cent tone of voice, and 10 per cent what is said. The Center for Creative Leadership's RACSR Model is a valuable approach. Each of the five stages in the Model provides a framework for how to approach a coaching session and improve your coaching technique and practice.

Build a relationship It is important to get to know your direct reports well or anyone else you are seeking to support. Questions that will help you establish the coaching boundaries, to get to know the person, understand who they are and what motivates them might include:

- 'How can we best work together?'
- 'What challenges are you facing that you would like to talk about?'
- 'Can you tell me more about your situation so I can understand it better?'

Remember to reflect back what you have heard and clarify that you have heard correctly.

Assessment The assessment stage is about helping the coachee understand themselves better. This stage can be inclusive of formal feedback, such as an appraisal outcome, or informally to help them reflect on how they performed in a recent situation. Questions you might consider asking include:

- 'What do you think about the feedback you received?'
- 'What was surprising for you?'
- 'With the power of hindsight, what might you have done differently?'
- 'What did you learn?'
- 'What do you want to do with what you have learnt?'

Providing feedback is an important part of the assessment stage because it helps promote insight and self-awareness. As you get to understand the person you are coaching, you will know how, and when, to best deliver feedback. If the person is not used to receiving feedback, or the feedback is not particularly positive, they will more than likely go through an 'emotional curve' as they react to it. This could cause them to have a variety of reactions and respond anywhere on the spectrum from shock and surprise, to anxiousness, anger or denial, before acceptance, and finally regaining hope. Your role as coach is to walk with the person through those stages, helping them to regain a sense of optimism.

Challenge The primary purpose of asking powerful questions is to challenge the coachee's current thinking and assumptions to help promote different behaviour. Questions that you can ask at this stage include:

- 'What are you currently doing, or not doing, that is getting in the way of you achieving your goals?'
- 'What is at risk for you?'
- 'What alternatives might you imagine?'
- 'What is the cost of not making the change?'
- 'What is the next step for you?'

Support Once the coachee has brainstormed a number of possible options and selected the one that should yield the best outcome, your role is to demonstrate that you are committed and invested in their development. You are not only helping the coachee to identify the resources that they need to make the change, or implement the action plan they have decided upon, you are asking them what you can do to help them remain committed to the goals they have set. Some questions you might consider asking include:

- 'How can I best support you?'
- 'What resources might you need to achieve your goals?'
- 'What may get in the way of you achieving success with this?'

Results Change, and therefore growth, won't occur unless specific goals are established, and the coachee understands that there is accountability for achieving them. The key to this step is helping the coachee develop realistic, achievable goals within a set timeframe. These could be a mixture of short-term goals (for example, things they will achieve before you next meet), and long-term goals (for example, goals that will help measure the success of a project or action).

Agree on the goals, performance indicators and timelines, and ask them to document what has been decided. Let them know that you will follow up with them at an agreed time. Questions that you could ask at this stage include:

- 'What will you begin to do differently? What will that look like?'
- 'How will you know when you have been successful?'
- 'What do you think will be the first change other people will notice?'
- 'How else can I help?'

Evaluate yourself Finally, the best way of improving your coaching skills is to ask the people you are coaching to give you feedback. The former head of People Analytics at Google recommends that leaders ask their people three questions:

- 'What is one thing I currently do that you'd like me to stop doing?'
- 'What is one thing that I currently do that you'd like me to do more often?'
- 'What can I do to help you be more effective and grow in your role?'

Alternatively, at the end of a formal coaching session it can be revealing to ask, 'Was that helpful?' If you have developed a constructive relationship with the person, they will have the courage to offer you helpful feedback to promote your own growth as a coach.

#9. CARING

'Love your neighbour as yourself.'

— Matthew 22:39

My first headship was as the founding principal of a new school in Australia's Capital Territory. It started small, with just 24 students and 2.2 staff members (two full-time people, and one part-time person). When I was appointed, the owners of the new school had just acquired the land: a barren sheep paddock located adjacent to where the new town centre would be built. (The only nearby buildings were a petrol station and a partially constructed Woolworths supermarket.) To create something from nothing was a remarkable experience. Selling a vision to people is much harder when there is literally nothing for people to see. In this instance, I was asking parents to entrust their children to a school that had no buildings, no resources, no staff and no finances.

As you can imagine, the first staff members and I got to know each other incredibly well. It is so much easier to extend care to an employee when you work closely with them. You know when they are having a bad day, or when they are stressed. You can share their grief, and their joy. You know their birthday and get invited to their wedding. The school grew relatively quickly, more than doubling in number each year. Now it is a place with more than 1500 students and well over 200 staff spread across two campuses.

What intrigued me the most when looking for leadership practices that engender trust was this practice: *caring*. It intrigued me because I undertook my research within large organisations – places with more than 140 staff members – because I wanted to identify the specific leadership practices, as opposed to character traits or personality types, that grow trust. Ultimately, trust is a relational (social) phenomenon – it is far easier to grow when you have opportunities to get to know people as individuals and not so easy when you are responsible for teams of hundreds or even thousands of people.

In my current role I have responsibility for well over 200 employees. One of the challenges I faced coming into this role was – how could I show care for each of them? When would I have the time? The remarkable results that came out of my research on highly trusted leaders, was that a majority of employees all believed they had a leader who genuinely cared.

They observed that care was extended by their leaders in very practical ways, including offering staff an empathetic ear, offering time off work to support a family member, follow-up conversations to check up on people, and permission to attend weddings and funerals. While not every member of staff had direct experience of the personal concern of the CEO, they nonetheless had heard of their authentic compassion for others. For these people the stories of care had led them to offer their trust to a leader who was compassionate towards those they were responsible for:

> 'I trust him implicitly. He cares for people. Some of the things that I see, that give me a really firm belief in him as a leader, is when I see everyday people walking into his office sometimes not feeling so good and they walk out feeling buoyed. He is a wonderfully affirming person. It really is a gift that he has.'

> 'If you have got any personal problems or whatever, he will be in touch. My husband is really sick at the moment and quite often [the Head] will ring and check up and see how he is. He cares ... and it's not just about caring for his staff, it's caring about the extended wellbeing of the people and it's just lovely.'

Why is *care* an important practice in building trust? Because when someone cares for you, you feel safe, you feel valued, you feel understood and you feel that you matter. A number of studies have confirmed the benefits of caring for employees. In his PhD Dissertation 'The Role of Caring Behavior and Peer Feedback in Creating Team Effectiveness', leading expert on group emotional intelligence Steven Wolff examined caring behaviours on team effectiveness. His work found that caring behaviours, such as expressing concern over wellbeing, understanding another's perspective, and speaking warmly to colleagues, generated a sense of safety and *trust*. The results of his study showed that caring behaviours had a direct impact on individual learning and performance, which then positively affected team outcomes.

In 2014 Sigal Barsade and Olivia O'Neill published a research paper titled: 'What's love got to do with it?' The study surveyed

3200 employees across seven industries. They found that employees who felt that they worked in a caring environment, where their wellbeing was considered important and they were valued as people, reported higher levels of job satisfaction, had less absenteeism, experienced less stress and were more productive. In the long-term care industry, one of the focuses of Barsade and O'Neill's study, cultures of care towards staff had a knock-on effect: employees took greater care of clients, improving patient mood and their quality of life, which resulted in fewer trips to the emergency room. Essentially, the more love (warmth, affection and connection) co-workers feel at work, the more engaged they are.

If I were to describe a person I trusted, I would talk about care. I will offer a person my total trust if I know that they genuinely care for me; only then will I open up and share my feelings with them. The odd thing about trust is that while I know it is vitally important for leadership, I reserve my offering of total trust to a select few. While I have no problem with trusting people to do their job, and no issue with being vulnerable or admitting my mistakes, I do struggle to let people into my personal world. Perhaps this is because I have been a leader for too long and have grown a healthy sense of scepticism about people's motives when they try to forge a friendship with me.

Finding a person to debrief with or share your innermost fears is very difficult. Tremendous care needs to be taken with the sensitive and confidential information you have been entrusted with, which often leaves you to carry some burdens on your own. This is why leadership is often described as a very lonely job.

The leadership practice of care is a reminder that ultimately companies are human organisations. People matter; people should come first. Relationships flourish when there is genuine care and concern extended to people. The central purpose of leadership is to serve the people who follow you. The leaders of the institutions where abuse occurred should have cared enough to believe what the children said or should have noticed when the light in their eyes began to dim.

WHEN IT ISN'T WORKING

On 21 August 2018, *The Australian* newspaper reprinted a short article headlined, 'We showed no care for children'. The Pope had issued a letter to Catholics around the world condemning the crime of priestly sexual abuse and cover-up. Pope Francis begged forgiveness for the pain and suffering caused by the Church. In his letter, the Pope said, 'We showed no care for the little ones; we abandoned them.' He went on to blast the culture of the Church where its leaders were more concerned for their reputation than the safety of children.

When abuse victim Archie published his blog on 10 October 2015, he used these words: 'Why have generations of abused kids had to suffer this crap, and been forced to live in fear, simply because a bunch of old school ties cared more about their wretched institution's reputation than they did about the welfare of the children.'

We all have an innate desire to belong to something bigger than ourselves. Sadly, this desire can persuade a leader into thinking that their sole responsibility is to protect the reputation of the organisation they work for. This can result in the CEO being perceived as callous, cold, calculated and uncaring by the individuals within the organisation. The desire to protect organisational reputation was the undoing of almost all the institutions under the spotlight in the Royal Commission into Institutional Responses to Child Sexual Abuse. In the years that the abuse occurred, the then leaders were perceived to have 'sided' with the perpetrators by 'covering up' their actions in the false belief that they were saving face. I cannot entirely imagine what they were thinking, but perhaps they thought a single casualty was worth the risk, that sweeping the crimes under the carpet was the best course of action. Perhaps they believed the perpetrator when they promised it would never happen again.

What caused many victims to become angry and bitter was the continual denial by the leaders of these organisations. For the victims, the covering up of the crimes was just as unforgivable as the crimes themselves. Left unchecked it led to the abuse of more children. As such, many victims carry a misplaced sense of guilt for not having done more. The victims had to fight to be heard, to be believed and to be acknowledged. For some that fight took decades. For others, that fight was too difficult.

Can a CEO offer care to an individual and protect the reputation of the organisation at the same time? Care at its poorest happens when a CEO puts reputation and profit before people.

WHEN IT IS WORKING

Hugh Mackay, in his book *The Good Life*, defines leadership as an example of the life lived for others: leadership is the ultimate form of service. Mackay's definition epitomises the notion of 'servant leadership', which at its heart defines leadership as valuing others above yourself. The practice of care is at its best when the leader places the needs of others before their own – it is the ultimate act of service.

It is only when a leader truly grasps this notion that their motivation and actions of care will be seen by others as *authentic* and they will become highly trusted. It is true that a leader, particularly of a large organisation, cannot possibly demonstrate acts of care to every single employee. But if they are modelling true servant leadership they become known as people who are compassionate, their values are reflected in their behaviours, and their response and actions are directed towards the people who genuinely need support.

At its best the practice of care can be seen in surprising contexts and in ways that you might not have considered. Our perception of the military is one of extreme discipline. Perhaps one of the first images that comes to mind when you think of the army is the drill sergeant yelling abuse at new recruits as he works to break their spirit. In a 2017 article 'The Caring Leader' published in *strategy+business* online, Augusto Giacoman, a director at PricewaterhouseCoopers in New York, recalls a sergeant major who had completed multiple deployments in places like Afghanistan and Baghdad. When he gave a command, his soldiers would respond with, 'How high?' What impressed Augusto and his fellow officers was how much the sergeant *cared*. When the sergeant major first joined the unit he gathered the officers together for a leadership training session. He played a video of the children's story *The Giving Tree*, the last thing you would imagine one of the toughest, hardened war veterans doing in front of a group of stern-faced officers. The story, by Shel Silverstein, describes the love of a tree (the main character) for a little boy (love in the story being what the ancient Greek's describe as *agape love*, an unconditional love that is bigger than ourselves, a boundless compassion and infinite empathy). In the story the tree gave and gave to the boy until there was no more to give – first his leaves, then his apples, and finally, when the boy had grown into a man, his trunk so he could make a boat to 'sail away and be happy'. After the video had ended the sergeant major uttered a simple, seven-word command to the officers: 'Be the Giving Tree to your soldiers.' The lesson to care for their soldiers more than themselves had a profound and lasting impact on Augusto.

When Lance Hockridge joined Aurizon, Australia's largest rail freight operator, as CEO in 2007, he brought an obsessive focus on prioritising worker safety. The reactions by investors was mixed. Whenever an investor briefing came around and he spoke about safety the most common reaction he received was, 'Yeah, yeah, we hear that, now get on with the important things.' But the reality was, Aurizon used to hurt too many people. His care of employees was expressed as a deep concern for their safety, particularly those employees who 'worked on the ground' in a very dangerous environment. His unrelenting focus on safety significantly reduced accidents; in the last two years of Hockridge's tenure as CEO there were no accidents serious enough for an employee to lose time at work. This was the single achievement that Hockridge was proudest of, despite the investment community taking little interest in safety as an indicator of good leadership. 'If you get that right, if you care about the people who work for you, then you have earned the right to manage your business.' The added benefit of caring for the people who worked for Aurizon was an increase in productivity – a win–win for everyone.

Much like Lance Hockridge, each highly trusted leader in my research into trust and leadership took the time to demonstrate a very real responsibility for people in their community. It began with knowing the names of their employees. These leaders had an extraordinary capacity to remember every staff member's name and also personal details, such as their family members and interests. As you undertake Practice #6: *Visibility*, occasions to develop relationships and learn about people's lives will result. Practising being visible provides opportunities to demonstrate care.

The wise opening words of David Brooks' 2015 book *The Road to Character* encourages us to pause and reflect:

> 'I've been thinking about the difference between resumé virtues and eulogy virtues. Resumé virtues are the ones you list on your resumé, the skills you bring to the job market and that contribute to external success. The eulogy virtues are deeper. They're the virtues that get talked about at your funeral, the ones that exist at the core of your being – whether you are kind, brave, honest or faithful; the type of relationships you formed.'

As I consider these words, I want to be remembered not as a successful man, but as a good man. Care at its best speaks to the source and motivation of a highly trusted leader's virtues and actions.

REFLECTION

I met David through Twitter. He started following me about six months after the royal commission hearing. His Twitter handle caught my attention: *#AbuseVictim*. His contact beckoned a response. There began three months of back-and-forth direct messaging until he finally agreed to reveal his identity.

#AbuseVictim hadn't been abused at the school at which I am now principal, but at another school where the counsellor had worked previously. David had suffered a total nervous breakdown when the royal commission was announced. He was living overseas at the time, having fled the country in an attempt to run from the memories that haunted his dreams. The media coverage brought suppressed feelings back to the surface.

#AbuseVictim was so affected by the trauma of the abuse that he lived in fear of his life. He believed that a paedophile ring had been operating that involved some very powerful and influential people – a conspiracy theory that, if true, could have far-reaching implications. After some weeks, *#AbuseVictim* agreed to communicate with me via email, but under another pseudonym. Some nights I would receive a dozen emails from him. It took many more weeks of listening and gaining his trust before he agreed to meet with me in person. He had returned to Australia because he had been disenfranchised by the institution he belonged to when he was a boy. His alienation was born out of the response to abuse victims of the school he attended. While his old school had done much to acknowledge the mistakes of the past and make recompense with the victims, it had not refunded any school fees to the victims. In his mind, his school didn't care enough.

The decision by the Archbishop responsible for my school to refund the fees to compensate the parents of abuse victims was controversial. It flew in the face of the advice of lawyers and was contrary to the policy of all the other institutions across the country. By refunding the fees, they were admitting liability. It was a full admission that the school had failed in its obligation to keep their children safe, it had failed in its duty of care. It also set a precedent for other schools to follow suit.

This posed a real conflict of ideology for the leaders of the other organisations involved in the comission hearings. How far do you extend care? What is realistic and fair? How do you balance the needs and reputation of the current community with the damage and hurt inflicted in the past?

In the end, David's old school decided not to refund the fees, deciding instead to offer recompense and care in other ways. Sadly, this didn't meet David's expectations and so he had reached out to me.

I was privileged to listen to David and to walk with him through some of his darkest moments, but I couldn't give him what he craved. We can value others above ourselves, offer genuine and authentic care, but sometimes those actions don't meet the needs of a person. Does this make you any less compassionate, less caring or trustworthy? We can control how we think, behave, and the decisions we make, but we cannot be responsible for how others choose to receive our offers of support. Sometimes our care isn't enough, or we cannot give what an individual most wants. Leaders are often caught between making decisions for the individual or for the greater good. For the leader who genuinely cares, these are the hardest decisions to make.

While I couldn't meet David's needs in full, a compassioned response to his pain helped David find a degree of peace. His connection to the school was the abuser; he shared the same story, a bond as it were, with our past students. It seemed right to ask him to participate in the designing of the sculpture garden and I invited him to contribute something for its opening. He responded by writing a poem, 'Stained-glass Spectacles.' The poem describes David's journey through pain and mental breakdown, but the final lines of the last stanza read:

Music box re-wound with a different tune;
Final lullaby, soft melody for resting weary lid.
Hope and glory to have faith,
For peace be finally with you all.

The backdrop for his words was the light of a single candle, lit in memory of those boys who suffered at his school, the flickering flame casting a warm glow on the plaque where his poem is permanently recorded. David's participation in the creation of *The Beginning of Peace* helped him regain a semblance of hope in humanity, so that he can trust again.

GETTING BETTER

It is a challenge to demonstrate the qualities of caring when you also need to be a strong and decisive leader who takes responsibility for an entire organisation. Some decisions that you make won't necessarily have the appearance of demonstrating care, especially when they impact directly on staff wellbeing and livelihoods. Your intentions – how you make those decisions and how you approach those affected – will ultimately shape people's perception of you. The following suggestions can help you on the path to including more care into your leadership role.

Learn people's names Your name is intimately personal, the key to your identity. It was given to you at birth and is reserved for those who know you. To everyone else, you are just another face in the crowd. Authentic care begins with knowing a person's name. When you first meet people, and until you know them well, use their full name. Shortened versions of someone's name, or nicknames, are reserved for closer associations. Care offered without that key is hollow. Highly trusted leaders know the power of learning people's names. It signifies the beginning of a relationship, a connection that grants a leader permission to offer genuine care when it is needed.

Build empathy As you get to know people, you can begin to get an insight into their needs. However, try to avoid making presumptions about people. Over time I have learnt that I can't always accurately predict how a person will react in a given situation, or what support will be most useful for them. Even though our intentions may be honourable, sometimes our offers of care can be insensitive because we aren't fully aware of a person's situation or story. Care begins with Practice #1: *Listening*. Often this is enough, but when it isn't, listening brings the empathy we need to make decisions about effective support.

Show compassion Some rules are hard and fast, while others can be flexible. A leader's role is not just to be the enforcer of the rules, but to exercise wisdom and compassion. For example, Award Agreements stipulate the amount of sick leave a person can take in any given year, but life doesn't follow rules. People get sick, sometimes for protracted periods, or they find themselves in a situation where they are the sole carer of a dying parent. An employee can be swamped by extraordinary circumstances causing considerable emotional, physical or financial stress, or even a combination of all three. To offer genuine care, a leader may have to bend the rules. One employee told me that for weeks following the inundation of her home by flood waters her CEO allowed her to leave work at 2 pm each day to help her to attend counselling, sort out the insurance claim, and to oversee the renovation of her home. When she needed it the most, support was given in a practical way without her pay or leave entitlements being impacted. She was eternally grateful and indebted to her employer for what he had done for her and her family.

Keep confidences The more you are trusted, the more people will share with you, looking to you as a source of wisdom and support. You will come into possession of the intimacies of individual lives. During the royal commission, I heard horrific stories, some shared publicly, some shared privately in my office. Great care has to be taken with the sensitive information you are entrusted with. A good strategy is always to ask people the question: 'Are you happy for me to tell others about this or would you rather no-one else know?'

Be consistent The hardest decisions a leader has to make are the ones that will result in individual casualties. Restructures, redundancies or terminations of employment are examples of the terrible dilemmas a highly trusted leader sometimes faces. For the greater good, a leader might have to let an individual go, or even hundreds of people. He or she knows that their decision will have a terrible impact on the lives of not just the employee who is about to lose their job, but also their families. A CEO is not a pastor, but a leader employed to make the hard decisions.

However, as difficult and as emotionally draining as these decisions are, care can still be extended to the affected person/s:

the offer of counselling and retraining, time off to attend interviews, assistance with putting together applications, or just occasional dropping in to see if they are okay. As hard as it is to face an employee after they have received difficult news, a leader who genuinely cares knows that they cannot hide. They still have a responsibility for the people affected by difficult decisions.

Deliver the bad news in person It takes enormous courage, but it is far more caring to deliver bad news in person than by email. Society frowns on those who 'break up' via text, so don't be the leader who lets a person know that they 'no longer have a position' in a letter. If people genuinely matter, then you will deliver difficult news face-to-face.

Be humble You aren't leading if no-one is following, and few people will willingly follow a person they know doesn't care. A good question to ask yourself is: 'Would people still follow me even if they didn't have to?' If there is some doubt in your ability to answer this question, then maybe you aren't an example of a compelling leader. The words of Paul the Apostle are powerful words, 'Do nothing out of selfish ambition or vain conceit. Rather, in humility value others above yourselves' (Philippians 2:3).

Care for yourself Caring for others can be incredibly rewarding but also exhausting. You cannot care for others when you are depleted of emotional energy. It is vitally important to take care of yourself. Ensure you get enough sleep, eat well and keep physically fit. When times are tougher than normal, ensure you have a confidante you can debrief with, or a trusted colleague who can share the load. Good counsellors have a supervisor, good leaders have a coach. They know that they are not immune to the effects of stress, or the immense responsibility for the lives of those they lead.

#10. KEEPING CONFIDENCES

'When others have entrusted a person with private or sensitive information they have a moral obligation to honour that trust; the breach of confidentiality may cost that relationship.'
— Reina and Reina

Why is it that people love to gossip? Knowledge is power and gives us identity, but it is power only if others know you are in possession of special information that no-one else has. The digital age has increased the risk of our confidential information being shared with others. In times gone by, we would hear the occasional story of people's medical records found fluttering in the wind at the local dump, but now we hear stories of people's personal information being dumped on the internet for anyone to access. The Information Security Newspaper website provides regular reports on breaches of confidential information. In May 2019 it reported that an IT services company had inadvertently exposed the passwords of its employees and, subsequently, their confidential employment information including their full names and phone numbers. The exposed data was of the type malicious hackers love to get hold of and sell to phishing campaigns.

Perhaps the most alarming and widely reported incident in recent times of confidential information being shared was the 2018 Facebook scandal. Up to 87 million Facebook users across the globe faced the possibility that their personal information was harvested by Cambridge Analytica, a British political consulting firm. It was later discovered that the data was used to build a software program to predict and influence voters in the 2016 US Federal Election. That same year it had also been used to influence the UK's Brexit vote. More alarming was that Facebook knew about the information being harvested in late 2015 but failed to alert users at the time. In a marathon hearing in the US Senate that lasted for more than five hours, Facebook's CEO, Mark Zuckerberg, agreed that people have a right to privacy, calling the 'incident' a breach of trust. As reported in *The Guardian* on 11 April 2018: 'I believe that it's important to tell people exactly how the information that they share on Facebook is going to be used.'

Zuckerberg had little choice but to take responsibility for the massive breech in data: 'It was my mistake, and I'm sorry. I started Facebook, I run it, and I'm responsible for what happens here.' The incident caused a $100 billion drop in Facebook's share price and triggered a review and tightening of online data protection regulations.

Facebook found itself in the spotlight again at the beginning of 2019 for another breach of confidentiality. In January 2019, a *Forbes* article titled 'Facebook has just been caught spying on users' private messages and data – again', reported an 'immense global backlash' following the revelation that Facebook planned to integrate its three messaging platforms, Messenger, WhatsApp and Instagram, into one giant data mining opportunity. Using an Application (app) disguised as a research project, Facebook had been caught paying young people for unfettered access to private data and personal messages. *Forbes* and other media outlets across the globe were outraged, positing that data exploitation had become so entrenched in the DNA of Facebook that it literally couldn't help itself but capitalise on what it saw as legitimate opportunities to further their business model. Following intense media attention, Facebook pulled the app that was allowing them access to people's personal messages and issued a statement renouncing the accusation of 'spying'. The saga was not unlike the phone hacking scandal by *News of the World* and other British newspapers, where employees used technology to listen in on people's phone conversations in pursuit of a story. Technology moves so fast that laws struggle to keep up.

But trust is a two-way street. Employees, not just the companies themselves or their leaders, can be found to breach confidences. Brisbane-based law firm, HR Law, published the outcome of a 2016 case brought by SAI Global Property Division against a former employee. Before the person's resignation in 2015 the staff member had copied two computer files containing highly sensitive confidential information to a USB device. The person then used that information for the benefit of their new employer, a direct competitor to SAI Global. The case ruled in favour of the plaintiff, with the former employee ordered to pay SAI Global $205,647 in damages. The ruling was a strong reminder to all involved about the importance of confidentiality.

When you are in a position of leadership, you become privy to sensitive information. While I am not responsible for a company as large as Facebook, nor do I possess information that has commercial value to others, I have learnt that it is a privilege to be invited into people's lives to hear their greatest joy, and despair. If you are genuinely trusted, people will share their innermost fears and concerns with you. This becomes a self-fulfilling cycle. The more you keep a person's confidence, the more you are trusted and, in turn, the more people will share with you. This brings the opportunity to walk with others and mentor or coach them. The reward is seeing a fellow human move out of despondency and into a place where they can flourish.

No experience of this cycle has been more powerful and compelling than the experience I had in the lead-up to the Royal Commission into Institutional Responses to Child Sexual Abuse. There is a fine line between keeping a confidence and passing on information that you are legally bound to disclose, but the lessons reinforced through those experiences are a reminder of how to keep confidences. More often than not, people just want to share the burden, they are not expecting you to act. If you genuinely want to grow trust, you need to be prepared to carry that burden with them in solitude.

With this privilege comes huge responsibility. Truly keeping confidences means that you forgo the power that knowledge can bring. To truly keep a person's confidence, you have to be comfortable in your own skin so your identity isn't caught up in what you know, but rather is measured by how much you are trusted. To be trustworthy, and true to this practice, you must always ask permission if you feel that the information you have been entrusted with needs to go further.

Keeping confidences is the most fundamental and obvious practice in building trust, but it is the practice that can most easily be a leader's undoing. If you breach a person's confidence without their permission it is incredibly hard, and in some cases impossible, to re-establish your credibility as a trusted leader.

WHEN IT ISN'T WORKING

We would hope that doctors would be the best at being tight-lipped, but not so. They are human, after all. Following 33,157 hours of observation in hospitals on the part of researchers at the University of Cordoba in Spain, it was found that there was at least one breach every 62.5 hours, or 2.6 days. Most of those breaches involved medical personnel disclosing personal data either intentionally or otherwise. Apart from the damage done to an individual medical practitioner's reputation, a breach in doctor–patient confidentiality can result in a person choosing not to seek medical help even in a critical situation.

In 2018 the Australian Government began a notification period for its new My Health Record site. Citizens were initially given a three-month window to 'opt out' of having their medical data stored 'securely' online, otherwise the government assumed that individuals were happy for their personal information to be kept on My Health. During the second half of 2018 there was intense debate about the proposed site and many Australians, deeply concerned about security and privacy, opted out.

At its worst this practice resembles gossip. Loose tongues revel in sharing information and use information to gain advantage and elevate their own sense of importance. For these people, knowledge is used to gain influence; they delight in knowing a little about everyone and being privy to information that others don't know. Yet there is nothing more hurtful than having your trust breached, or to discover that something you shared in confidence has been shared with others. Even one careless breach of a confidence can taint a leader's, a company's or a government's, reputation, causing others to hesitate in sharing information, both personal and professional. When this happens, people begin to withdraw from the leader and information is held close. Fear begins to creep its way into the culture of the organisation.

I learnt a powerful lesson early in my tenure as principal. An employee, Jane, made an appointment to see me during which she shared the frustrations she had with working with a colleague. She told me that the situation had become so challenging for her that she was losing sleep and was considering leaving the organisation. She was an excellent hire and I didn't want to lose her, so I met with her colleague and confronted her with Jane's concerns. Jane found out and was furious with me. She hadn't wanted me to do anything about her frustrations at that point; she had just wanted to make me aware of what was going on and to let me know how she was feeling. My poor decision had a lasting impact as she decided to resign. The incident probably also damaged other people's trust in me, including her colleague.

WHEN IT IS WORKING

In most modern workplaces there are two types, or levels, of confidentiality. There are formal agreements where many companies, like SAI Global, have specific confidentiality clauses written into employment contracts to protect their commercial interest. Then there are relational obligations, when leaders and work colleagues come into possession of information that affects individuals on a more personal level.

The doctor–patient relationship is probably the best example of an individual coming into possession of potentially sensitive information. We go to a doctor when we need help and rely heavily on their willingness to keep our details private. Medical practitioners are said to be bound by the Hippocratic oath, whereby doctors swear to uphold ethical standards, including medical confidentiality. This gives us a high degree of confidence to share our intimate details, safe in the knowledge that they won't pass them on to anyone else without our consent. The trust in this relationship is often so strong that people disclose more to their doctor than they do to their partner.

Employees working for the highly trusted leaders in my research project on trust leadership knew that they could share personal information with their CEO, safe in the knowledge that unless permission was granted, the information would not go any further. As one employee reports:

> 'You won't find that she has betrayed your confidence. Well, I have never found that she has betrayed a confidence where I have had some of those difficult discussions and then found [out] that somebody has told me back part of that discussion … I feel that I can have faith in her that I can have a [confidential] discussion.'

The keeping of confidences is at its best when the leader is confident and content in who they are. Their identity is not associated with power or position, and they are motivated by a higher purpose – to make a difference in other people's lives. That self-assurance and outward focus makes 'keeping mum' far easier when they come into possession of sensitive information.

Highly trusted leaders know that they are responsible not only for the individual, but also for the collective. Sometimes the new knowledge they are given requires a response, perhaps even an urgent one. To do nothing could be irresponsible. When these circumstances arise, a highly trusted leader will seek permission from the sharer to act before they do anything; or they empower the sharer by bringing him/her into their confidence and explain why and how they are going to act.

REFLECTION

When it comes to the safety and wellbeing of children mandatory reporting laws in Australia require certain individuals to report concerns to authorities immediately. But what of the information that has been disclosed to you by an adult in confidence?

The Royal Commission into Institutional Responses to Child Sexual Abuse concluded at the end of 2017. In all, the Commissioner handed down 409 recommendations aimed at keeping children safe. The most contentious was the recommendation to open the confessional so that religious ministers should be forced to report information confided to them during confession. The recommendation called for the confidentiality of a centuries-old sacrament to be breached.

The Catechism of the Catholic Church at section 1456 states that 'Confession to a priest is an essential part of Penance.' The intent of the sacrament is to provide healing for the soul of the person confessing their sin. To demonstrate true penitence, the confession is not made in secrecy, nor to a friend, layman or other human authority, but to an ordained priest; the Catholic Church believing that an ordained priest has the authority of God to announce the forgiveness of sins. Key to the sacrament of the confessional is the *seal*, or confidentiality.

In 2010 the Vatican's Congregation for the Doctrine of the Faith gave permission to bishops to report child sexual abuse by clergy, but only where there was civil and/or criminal mandatory reporting law. It is now compulsory in every state of Australia for priests to disclose abuse on the part of other priests or Church workers. However, for the Church, the sacrament of Penance is a different issue, a holy and theological matter.

Australian states responded to the royal commission's 2017 recommendation to break the seal of that confessional by drawing up legislation that would override Church Canon Law making it compulsory for priests to disclose abuse crimes told in the confessional by any person. The royal commission noted in their final report that religious freedom cannot be absolute: 'Governments legislate for the common good, for all citizens. They must not be thwarted by customs or laws of particular religions which could threaten the common good.' In response, the leaders of several Archdioceses said that they would instruct priests to defy the law of the land and uphold the law of God.

To tell or not to tell? To uphold a centuries-old sacrament and the 'innate superiority of the Church,' or obey the common law of the land? Should any person with knowledge concerning the safety of an innocent child be exempted from a moral and legal obligation to report to the civil authorities?

The predicament for the Catholic Church is compounded by the overwhelming evidence that abusers within its ranks were protected and continued to commit their crimes unabated for decades. From the outside, the Catholic Church's response to the royal commission's recommendation to open the confessional gives the appearance that it has learnt little from its massive failure to keep the innocent and vulnerable safe.

Dissenters to the proposed legislation argue that the changes would not be effective in making it safer for children.

They claim that few paedophiles go to confession; that by nature of the confessional their identity is typically hidden from the priest; and, they might not confess if they knew that the seal did not apply. Many Church leaders see no need to review Canon Law in light of the Commission's findings and recommendations.

I am not a priest and so I don't have to wrestle with this conflict. But I am a teacher, and as such, am bound by mandatory reporting legislation. Under Queensland's *Child Protection Act 1999* teachers, as well as doctors and nurses, are bound by law to report a reasonable suspicion that a child is in need of protection caused by any form of abuse or neglect. I have never had a situation where an adult has confided in me that he or she was harming a child, although I have had to make mandatory reports on many occasions.

I do, however, come into possession of other challenging information that is shared in confidence. One victim wrote to me with these words:

'I hate myself. I'm a disgrace. I'm totally fucked up. I've done some terrible shit; so many terrible things. I wish I was in prison, or dead. I would like to tell you my life story and confess my sin to you. To help you understand why I did the shit I did.'

The person in question had been barraging me with correspondence for several weeks but it wasn't until after this particular message that we met face-to-face. As I went into the conversation I knew I needed to listen with compassion but that I might need to make a judgement about what I did with the information I became privy to.

I have come to learn over the years that most people who share their story or frustrations with a colleague just want to vent to someone they trust. I have learnt that the best strategy to employ after someone has told you their worries is to ask them the question: 'Do you want me to do something about this or are you just telling me so I can understand?' I learnt this strategy after my powerful lesson with Jane.

However, since learning this strategy I have had to add another layer of practice when it comes to confidences. What if a person, in sharing a confidence with me, tells me information that places them or another person at risk? What if they tell me they have broken the law?

Ultimately, as a leader I have a duty of care to the people and the organisation I have been entrusted with. During the royal commission hearing a member of the community told me a story about the abuse they suffered in another state. Not only that, they shared with me a horrific story about the deaths of a number of friends. Were these unsolved murders? I had no idea.

I have resolved that in situations like the above I have no choice but to act upon the information I have received. It is not morally right to keep it confidential. When I do need to break a person's confidence I always tell them upfront what I am going to do and why. Most people have understood and accepted my decision, very few have been angry.

When that person from the community gave me information about possible crimes committed over four decades ago I told them that I had no choice but to tell the police. However, in doing so I empowered them in the process. I committed to letting them know when I had spoken with authorities, and that I would share their response.

This is an extreme example. There are lesser instances where I have had to breach a person's confidence, times when a person is in need of medical or specialist help, or when others are at risk of harm if I fail to act on information I have received. There is a fine line between keeping confidences and protecting others. Occasionally, a leader is called to make a decision that puts at risk a person's trust in you.

GETTING BETTER

The keeping of confidences is perhaps the most obvious and simplest of the trust-building practices. It is also the one that can undermine and destroy trust if not practised properly. For some people it is very hard to keep sensitive information private. When observing the following practical steps for protecting people's privacy, keep in mind the golden rule – always treat others the way you would like to be treated.

Ask questions When information is shared with you, it is good practice to ask the question: 'Are you telling me this because you need to share, or do you want me to do something about it?' Don't assume to know the expectations of others. In most instances, someone will share information with you because they trust you as a confidante, they do not necessarily expect you to action a response. However, sometimes the information is important enough to warrant action. When someone shares concerning information with you, ask yourself the questions:

- Is the wellbeing of the person sharing information best served by keeping this information confidential?

- Is anyone else at risk if nothing is done about what I now know?

Sometimes the wellbeing of the many outweighs the importance of staying silent. If you do decide to take action, you should inform the people involved that you are obliged to do something about what they have told you, either because you are legally obligated, or because their own and/or the wellbeing of others is better served by responding. While you are effectively breaching their confidence, the negative impact on trust is lessened by having explained your reasons. In most instances, people will forgive you when they understand your position. Even if they don't forgive you, the safety of others far outweighs the importance of your reputation as a trustworthy leader.

What is your identity? Knowing who you are and understanding the driving force or emotion behind your motivation will help enormously when it comes to keeping confidences. Do you experience an overwhelming desire to share information or do you have absolutely no urge to tell? If there is the urge to tell others, or even to give a hint that you know something they don't, you will have to work especially hard at this practice. Spend time in reflection to get in better touch with your values. It may be that your sense of identity is misplaced, that you gain a feeling of self-worth and importance because of the value of information people share with you, rather than by how much people trust you. If so, this will make it more difficult to become the trustworthy leader you aspire to be.

Be your confidante Who do you trust with your inner-most private thoughts and concerns? We all crave the friendship of a highly trusted person, and we know instinctively or through first-hand experience, who we can share information with and when we need to be more reserved. Placing yourself in the other person's shoes is a good way to remind yourself about what's at stake for others. Be your most trusted confidante to them. If you can't do that, then don't invite the person to share any more than they need to. Better not to be the recipient of confidential information than risk the temptation to share it. If you are struggling with the boundaries then use your own confidante as a sounding board, being careful not to wander into gossip territory by giving away identities.

Write it down I have sometimes found it helpful to record important information. Our memory can exaggerate the information that it receives, or catastrophise it. Noting the detail helps focus on the specifics and can help you maintain your perspective as you piece together a full picture. Recording the information can also help guide you through a decision-making process about whether or not you need to act on what you have been told. It goes without saying that you need to ensure you keep all records of conversations secure.

TRUST RESTORED

repentance *noun,* the action of repenting; sincere regret or remorse.

CHANGING CULTURE

'Everyone thinks of changing the world, but no one thinks of changing himself.'

— Leo Tolstoy

There is a common notion that we all have an emotional bank account, or trust account: the more deposits we add to that account, the more we are trusted. A myth is then promulgated about trust – once we have built up a healthy account, it is okay if we make the occasional withdrawal. Another expression is similarly used to justify people's actions: 'It is easier to ask forgiveness than seek permission.' However, this implies that when your account is healthy you can deliberately do something untrustworthy. It assumes that people can be easily manipulated and that they will forgive you because, for the most part, you are trustworthy. This thinking is flawed as these behaviours inevitably damage perceptions of your integrity as a leader and people will lose trust in you as a result.

As we have discussed, trust is a socially constructed

phenomenon. It means different things to different people. To one person it will be all about confidences, to another it will be about the level of care extended to them. Trust is not like building credit. You can't expect to make a withdrawal and then save up again when you need. Trust is all about who we are, what we value, how we act and behave, and how we bring the qualities of honesty, reliability and integrity to our leadership. But no-one is perfect. The reality is that you will breach someone's trust at some point: a careless oversight, a thoughtless decision or action, a weak moment, or a deliberate withdrawal from the 'account'. When this does happen, people may be willing to forgive you if the breach was accidental, but far less so if it was intentional. In these cases, the path back to trust can seem impossible.

There are many ways that trust is diminished within organisations: inattention, thoughtlessness, lying, cheating, incompetence, deceit, narcissism, criminal activity. Many leaders couldn't conceive of the possibility that people don't trust them. Their own inflated view of themselves conveniently obscures the truth. Others just don't care. You might be forgiven for thinking that these words came out of their mouth: 'Of course, I'm not a narcissist … I'm way too amazing!' Their leadership is driven by their own egotistical need for power and admiration. Greed and arrogance lead them to use manipulation and fear as powerful methods to control people and get what they want.

Many people will have experienced this kind of leadership in their workplace. James was one such person who found himself working for an untrustworthy leader. Demoralised, and anxious about the impact the experience was having on himself and his family, James emailed me out of the blue. As I soon discovered, with the desire to give his young family the adventure of a lifetime,

James had accepted a two-year secondment to work in another country. However, a few months into the job he found himself in a toxic work environment and began to regret his decision. He had been following my work on trust and leadership for some time and sent me the following correspondence.

Dear Paul,

My name is James. I am an ex-pat currently working in Bangkok, Thailand for a relatively new business. I write to you with some concerns I have around the culture that has quickly been established in the organisation. Unfortunately, we have a leadership team who are using fear and coercion to drive the business. Many of the staff are angry and this anger has transformed into a toxic tension, which is destroying any hope we had of becoming a highly trusted organisation. I am not giving up and I write to you today to share my story and seek advice if you have the time to listen.

Currently, the leadership team is heavily focused on its core objectives, but unfortunately, they have totally ignored staff morale and the importance of trust. We are not a big company. In the past six months, two people have gone on stress leave and a wave of discontent is filtering through the remainder of the staff. I read somewhere that 'culture eats strategy for breakfast' and the more I think about this and spend time in this business I begin to understand just how true those words are.

The leadership team are more concerned about profit and pretending to be something they are not. Our website is deceptive. The difference between what is said about our product and the reality is stark, and I find it very hard not to say something. It appears the 'brand' is far more important than the human condition, which to me, is devastating. I approached one of the Directors with my concerns around the culture and her reply was that she was 'powerless to do anything'. The reason she gave to me for this 'lack of power' is that she is female and the CEO is male and any attempt to question his authority would be 'career suicide' on her part.

I find myself working in a business where we have a leader whom no-one trusts. In fact, and this is only my opinion, I very much doubt this CEO would tick any of the 10 practices of a highly trusted leader. I have, up until this time, focused on my work, trying to deliver high quality outcomes, but the climate here is toxic and many of the staff are unhappy. The Directors, of which there are three, are frustrated at what they need to deal with and this is permeating the entire organisation.

I am torn as to what to do. I know what it could be like. Should I sit back and focus solely on my work, or should I step in and try to cultivate change? How do you go about changing the culture if you have a leader who is not trusted? Your simple but profound statement on Twitter that 'good organisations are built on great relationships' is so true, and I just wish our leader could see this. My only other option is to leave.

Kind regards,

James

So, what do you do when distrust has cemented itself into the culture of the organisation and is played out in the norms and practices of the everyday routines and interactions of employees?

In September 2018, *The Australian* carried a news story about the preliminary findings of the banking royal commission. It found that the Commonwealth Bank of Australia (CBA) wilfully breached superannuation law more than 13,000 times. As the newspaper stated: 'The banking industry has embarked on an advertising blitz in an attempt to repair its battered reputation.'

Like most CBA customers, I received a letter from the new CEO, Matt Comyn, that same month. The letter stated the CBA's intention to restore trust: 'I'm sorry for the mistakes we've made. My job now is to fix them.' The long and arduous journey had begun for the bank to return to the values that the previous CEO had promulgated in the CBA's 2017 vision document, which claimed that trust was CBA's most important asset: 'Our stakeholders' trust in us rests on our honesty, capability and genuine concern for their financial wellbeing.'

Unfortunately, for leaders who are genuinely interested in others, there is a terrible paradox when it comes to trust. It is the condition that allows people and organisations to flourish but it can also be used as a tool to allow a person to commit atrocities. Trust was espoused as a core value of the CBA, but unscrupulous activity was allowed to continue unchecked until there was the political will to call into question the practices of many of Australia's financial institutions. In addition to the criminality and its effects, people who wield power can also use trust to craft a story to justify their criminal actions and manipulate those around them.

This, then, is the paradox for a leader of integrity: to be trustworthy but to be wise in how much they extend trust to others. A wise leader does not trust blindly. A wise leader listens carefully to all the 'noise' around them before making a decision about the level of trust they will offer another person. Comyn's letter of apology was a pivotal step in the process for restoring trust but it wasn't the most important. The first step to restoration of trust, is to *listen*.

Listening is much harder than talking, because listening involves a deliberate effort of will. It requires us to set aside the things we would rather be thinking about, or our preconceived notions about ourselves and others, and focus exclusively on what others are saying to us. The sound may come to the ears of the leader as a noisy gong or clanging cymbal. This was the case for the banks and the institutions responsible for protecting children exposed at the royal commissions, the noise became so loud they could no longer ignore the outcry. Other times the sound will come as a gentle whisper, a simple averting of the eyes suggesting that a person does not want to engage with you on any level because of their loss of trust in you. However loud or soft that sound comes, a leader who is genuinely concerned about trust and its restoration must humble themselves to listen. In the words of Hugh Mackay in his 2013 book *The Good Life*, 'Humility doesn't involve flagellating yourself, demeaning yourself or losing your self-respect; it involves only shifting your primary focus from your own wellbeing to the wellbeing of others.'

If James, working in the fledgling business based in Thailand, is willing to risk employment for his integrity, he could take his concerns directly to the person who needs to hear it the most: the CEO. He tried one director, but her hands were tied by the chauvinism of the leader. One can only hope that this leader will have the humility to listen. Unfortunately for James, I fear that it is more likely the CEO is not only *unaware* of the impact his leadership practice is having, but also won't want to *hear otherwise*.

Perhaps there was an employee somewhere in the CBA willing to question the bank's unlawful practices, but it would seem from the media reports that the CBA began listening only when there was no way out, and especially when their practices were exposed on the front pages of newspapers. Nonetheless, the listening had begun. And it began with humility. The new CEO took ownership of the mistakes and apologised unreservedly in a letter to every customer.

Similarly, during the 1980s and 1990s the principal of St Paul's, where over 120 boys were abused, failed to engender trust. Many of those students and their parents told the Royal Commission into Institutional Responses to Child Sexual Abuse that they had said something to the principal at the time, but he either failed to listen or chose not to act. The same can be said for countless other institutions across the country who had to front the royal commission and give evidence as to their failings to keep safe those young people entrusted to their care.

The most prolific paedophile at the school in this story used trust to his advantage. As the school's counsellor, he was meant to be one of the most trusted people on staff; the confidant, the person children shared their inner-most thoughts and fears with. But the counsellor wilfully hid behind practices of confidentiality and privacy to manipulate those around him. He used his charm and meek appearance to create a façade for the evil that lurked behind the locked door of his rooms. He peddled stories to draw his prey into his den. When they were sufficiently groomed, boys were abused over and over again. The crimes stopped only when one young victim, wearing a police wire, confronted the counsellor at his home. Knowing that the game was up, the counsellor chose the coward's way out: a bottle of whiskey to dull the smell of car exhaust fumes.

The final report of the Royal Commission into Institutional Responses to Child Sexual Abuse was handed down in December 2017. It followed five years of disturbing public hearings and resulted in thousands of pages of findings and recommendations. Suffice to say, it rocked the entire community as people began to understand the breadth and depth of the issue of child sexual abuse that had occurred within institutions across the country for decades.

On Monday 22 October 2018 in the Great Hall of Parliament House, the Prime Minister of Australia, grasping the hand of Cheryl Edwardes, the Chair of the National Apology Reference Group, read out a heart-wrenching apology to the victims of sexual abuse. As an act of unity, the leader of the Opposition held Cheryl's right hand. Survivors welcomed the apology, many stating that they had waited for years to be believed, to be acknowledged. For many, the event marked the beginning of healing.

Not all who attended the National Apology to abuse victims could be in the Great Hall. Many witnessed the event on the lawns outside Parliament House. When interviewing survivors for that evening's news bulletin, one ABC reporter was surprised by cynical responses: 'I have heard apologies before, they are all hollow because nothing happens from there.'

To truly admit your mistakes and restore trust, you need to walk in solidarity with those who were wronged. You cannot understand the impact of your mistake unless you can enter the other person's world and see the injustice from their point of view. In the words of award-winning journalist Greg Sheridan: 'Human solidarity is the willingness to share in another person's suffering when we might avoid it. It can be as simple as sitting with a spouse or a child who is sick, the most basic of elements of human solidarity. To express such solidarity with people beyond those we are naturally fond of is more difficult.'

For many companies that have experienced a critical failure in leadership the journey back to trust can often begin only with the appointment of a new CEO. This was certainly the case for the school in this story and for financial institutions in the banking royal commission spotlight, such as AMP. But a new CEO cannot ignore the past or shift the blame. They cannot make excuses or offer glib statements to the effect of, 'It's different now, that was all in the past.'

Only by accepting responsibility will a leader understand what needs to change to restore trust. Where there has been critical leadership failure, changes need to cut to the heart of the organisation. They need to challenge the existing norms and practices of the prevailing culture that allowed any malpractice to occur unchecked.

Confronting and changing company culture isn't easy, particularly in large organisations. When a group of people come together to form an organisation, or community, it is like birthing a new organism; social or crowd psychology comes into play. Written and unwritten norms are established, which govern how people behave. You only need attend a major sporting event or concert to experience the phenomenon of a crowd taking on a life of its own; people uniting and behaving in ways that they wouldn't usually behave if they were on their own.

Many leaders underestimate the power of the prevailing culture, particularly newly appointed leaders. The influence of a pernicious leadership style, especially following a long tenure, can mean that these unwritten norms become ingrained. A culture of mistrust can be hard to identify, and even harder to change. The oft-quoted saying, 'culture eats strategy for breakfast', is attributed to the late Peter Drucker, management consultant, educator and author. Many leaders have aspirations for an organisation's strategic vision but totally underestimate what people inside the organisation believe and how they behave. It is culture that often determines what happens in the workplace.

It is very hard to act in a counter-cultural way, particularly when our innate desire to fit in is subconsciously encouraging us not to push back against prevailing norms. No-one wants to be isolated from the group. Through a process of socialisation, many leaders find themselves enslaved by these often unspoken rules; and become conditioned to accept 'the way things are done around here'.

If you are a newly appointed leader coming into an organisation that has been haemorrhaging trust, it is important to remember that culture takes time to shift, but with integrity and effort it can shift. According to well-respected behavioural scientist Daniel Goleman, 70 per cent of an organisation's culture is influenced by the leader. If this is true, then you have the greatest position and privilege to change it. Using that influence to create a culture of trust can repair the damage within organisations in tangible ways.

For newly appointed leaders, there are five things that could help you wrestle the invisible beast (culture). The following strategies draw on my experience of coming into a culture of mistrust and changing the organisational direction to create a new identity and reputation for the business.

Seek to understand the prevailing culture Spend time listening and ask challenging questions of your staff to get an understanding of why things are done the way they are. What historical events, personalities and thinking influenced the current cultural norms? What, if anything, was tried before to address these issues, and why did these efforts fail? Take the time to identify the actions, behaviours and processes that you don't agree with and have the courage to lead a life that is in opposition to those things. People will see that you are different. Be true to your values and beliefs.

Identify the crusaders, the influencers and the naysayers There is a 60-30 rule of thumb. If 30 per cent of staff are with you (the crusaders) and 30 per cent are ambivalent, then you will have the majority to succeed. Don't waste your energy on the 30 per cent who will resist your change efforts.

However, if you can turn around one or two naysayers, particularly the ones who everyone looks to for advice or who have some influence in the organisation, then you are more likely to gain momentum. A good strategy is to draw a naysayer into your confidence and seek their opinion on some of the things you are considering. This not only demonstrates that you value their views but shows that you are willing to offer them trust even though they may not yet trust you. Alternatively, once you understand what motivates a naysayer, see if you can realign their role with their passions to help re-ignite their commitment to the organisation.

Resist the prevailing culture One way to avoid being subsumed into the existing culture is to write a list of the standard or expected social behaviours that you want to change within the organisation and a list of the ones you want to adopt. Post your list on a wall near your desk as a reminder of your goals for the organisation. Examples might include (as in the case of the CEO of the PR firm who would email the team when a person had made an error), a reminder that a growth mindset culture is the goal and includes establishing a program of coaching to build capacity. Or, if people only communicate via email and rarely build relationships, your goal might be to get out of the office to speak with people personally, to model different ways of communicating to help build and sustain a culture of trust.

Develop strategies to change the culture You can do this by setting up teams to oversee projects or specific tasks. Some of these might be to develop a new statement of beliefs or corporate philosophy. You may choose to start a tradition for acknowledging staff, or establish new processes for staff to provide feedback. Empower those teams to do the work but give them direction so they are working towards the goals you want to achieve. Putting a naysayer or influencer on those teams can be powerful if you select them wisely. Done well, this will help build motivation in people who may be more likely to resist change, although it is important not to rush to decisions about their inclusion or involvement. Like a good carpenter, measure twice and cut once.

Once a new strategy or norm is established, commit It takes time to embed a new way of working, so persevere. Commit to the timelines you have set to undertake an evaluation of the initiative and its impact. Resist the urge to give into the pleas of people who are struggling with change. It never ceases to surprise me that even though people have been invited to be part of the solution and agreed to decisions, it's not until a change initiative has been implemented that they realise the change is actually going to impact them. Most innovations fail, not because they were a bad idea, but because people gave up too early.

AUTHOR'S NOTE

The royal commission was not something that I ever expected when I was appointed as the Principal of St Paul's, but I know that one of my most important roles as leader is to establish, nurture and grow a culture that enables people to flourish and so I had to accept every responsibility that came with the appointment. While my experience was confronting, it was a privilege to share just a little of the journey of those who were so terribly wronged while they were students at the school in the 1980s and 1990s. The crimes that occurred should never have happened, and much has been done to ensure that, to the best of our ability, they will never occur again. The experience has helped me become a better person, a better leader, and I thank those who shared their lives with me to enable that to happen. I tell this story partly to highlight the importance of trust and how to restore and grow it, but more importantly, I tell this story to highlight the terrible scourge on our society that is sexual abuse. We mustn't let it continue.

The stories in this book may be seen as a breach of confidentiality. I have been given permission to share some of Archie's story, and to protect the identity of certain individuals

I have changed names and details. Telling their stories is an extreme example of trust destroyed, one that I hope acts as a reminder of what can happen when leaders fail to attend to their central responsibility, to attend to the wellbeing of the people they are entrusted to serve. At a time when they were at their most vulnerable, young people were robbed of their innocence and their childhood. When they should have been cared for, kept safe, listened to, believed and trusted, those in authority let them down in ways that changed their lives forever, setting many on a course of addiction, self-harm, failed relationships, imprisonment, and a constant pain that for many was too much to bear.

Post-traumatic stress disorder is the most common outcome for a person who has been sexually abused. It is a life sentence of fear, anxiety and depression as well as less recognisable symptoms, such as avoiding unfamiliar people, locations or circumstances and displaying high levels of sensitivity to certain people and confrontational situations.

During the five-year inquiry, the Royal Commission into Institutional Responses to Child Sexual Abuse was contacted by 16,953 people and they listened to 7981 individuals in 8013 private sessions. In addition to this, the Commission received 1344 written accounts. Of those survivors on record, 58 per cent said that the abuse they experienced took place in an institution managed by a religious organisation, 32.5 per cent said it took place in a government-run institution and 10.5 per cent in a non-government, non-religious institution.

Of those who were abused in a religious institution, the majority (61.4 per cent) claimed that they were abused in a Catholic Church institution, followed by an Anglican Church institution (14.8 per cent). These figures included church-owned schools. Almost two in three survivors were male. The average

age of survivors attending the private inquiry sessions was 52. For many, this was the first time they had ever talked about the abuse they had experienced as children. The oldest survivor to share their story at the Commission was 93 and the youngest was seven. Of the survivors who told their stories in private sessions 93.3 per cent said that they were abused by one or more male perpetrators. Some said that they were abused by several offenders, including offenders who were under the age of 18. One-third said that they were abused by a person in religious ministry and one in five said that they were abused by a teacher. The average age of victims when they were first abused was 10.4 years for male victims and 9.7 years for female victims.

Looking back, does this story say that schools and churches were uniquely bad? In one sense, sadly not. They may have hidden the most prolific paedophiles, but police figures suggest the vast majority of abuse of children occurs at home. Figures from the Australian Institute of Family Studies, 2017, have measured the prevalence of child sexual abuse and found that 1.4–7.5 per cent of all boys are victims of penetrative sexual abuse and 5.2–12 per cent are victims of non-penetrative abuse; 4.0–12.0 per cent of girls are victims of penetrative sexual abuse and 14–26.8 per cent are victims of non-penetrative abuse. Most of this abuse occurs in and around the home and is committed by someone known and trusted — often loved.

According to these statistics, the abuse that occurred in institutions is only the tip of the iceberg. During the 2015–16 financial year there were 225,487 Australian children suspected of being harmed or at risk of harm from abuse/neglect. These figures are a sad indictment on our society.

What does this mean for me, and for others in leadership roles, particularly in organisations that have responsibility for children? Firstly, it means that we should ensure that we have systems, policies and practices in place to protect the vulnerable. We should always be vigilant, and we should listen and value the voice of children. Secondly, as leaders we should continually be conscious of our impact on the organisation and people we lead. Nothing is more important than creating and growing a culture of trust, both for the enabling of people and the empowerment of those who have been victimised. Once trust is broken, it is incredibly difficult to restore. For organisations, unless the current leader has the courage to humble themselves and seek forgiveness, the restoration of trust can often begin only with a change in leadership.

The journey to restoration starts with a concerted effort to listen, an honest desire to understand how trust was lost and what impact the breach in trust has had on people. Only then can a leader walk humbly in solidarity with those affected and be truly ready to give a frank and meaningful apology when the time is right. Atonement is only genuine when real and lasting change is made to demonstrate that the mistake will never happen again. In an organisation's case, that change must cut to the heart of the issue, the organisation's culture. If it is about broken trust in you, the changes necessary for atonement must begin with your behaviour and leadership practice; which of the ten trust-building practices let you down?

Listen carefully. Make the change and make it permanent.

APPENDIX: A STUDY IN TRUST

It was a shock to go from an environment of high trust to one where it was all but absent. I had enjoyed all that a culture of trust affords a leader and the impact it had on that organisation's ability to achieve its strategic goals. You don't notice the value of trust until it is missing. It was missing from the organisation I had joined and was severely impeding its ability to move forward in a positive way. This experience caused me to spend considerable time reflecting on my own leadership and how my behaviours might effectively and positively impact organisational culture. Following copious amounts of reading I embarked on a PhD with the Queensland University of Technology (QUT) to identify specific practices that highly trusted transformational leaders use to effectively inspire, build and maintain a relationship of trust with their staff and Chair of the governing body. The research design to achieve this aim was a qualitative, multi-case study.

The study was divided into two distinct phases: the first, the identification of four highly trusted transformational leaders; and, the second, a study of those leaders in situ. This was followed by a cross-case analysis of the four leaders. The outcome was the identification of 10 key trust-building leadership practices.

The study needed to be placed in a theoretical construct, or definition of leadership. Leadership is most often defined as the process of influencing people – by providing purpose, direction, and motivation – while operating to accomplish the mission and improving the organisation. But leadership, like trust, is a socially constructed phenomenon, and as such, you cannot have a single agreed definition. An internet search will return well over 30,000 descriptions of 'leadership' or 'leadership styles'.

The term 'leadership style', was first coined by three researchers in *The Journal of Social Psychology* in 1939, Lewin, Lippit and White. In their article, 'Patterns of aggressive behavior in experimentally created "social climates"' they referred to a range of different leadership constructs including, but not limited to: transactional, collaborative, consultative, autocratic, servant leadership, instructional leadership and transformational. I made the decision to base the study on the theory of transformational leadership. The late James Burns, an American historian, political scientist and author of the 1978 book *Leadership*, was the first to put a label on this style of leadership. He said that such leadership occurs when one or more persons engage with others in such a way that leaders and followers raise one another to higher levels of motivation and morality. Bernard Bass, academic and author of the 1985 book *Leadership and performance beyond expectations*, built on Burns's ideas about transformation leadership, defining the style in terms of articulating a compelling vision for followers. In other words, transformational leadership also energises people by providing them with an exciting vision for the future rather than using rewards and punishments. It occurs when leaders and followers are united in their pursuit of higher-level goals, which are common to both.

The work on transformational leadership sat well with me. I believe that a person isn't leading unless they are seeking to fulfil a vision, transforming or changing what an organisation currently is into something different. If a person isn't doing this, then they are just *managing* the status quo. Ultimately, leadership is about inspiring and supporting people to become better. When this occurs collectively, an organisation can not only reach greater heights but also innovate, a vital trait for companies if they want to survive in a world that is seeing an increasing rate of change.

Phase One of the study was a search for highly trusted transformational leaders. These were selected from the independent education sector. In Australia there are three providers of 'public' education: the government, the Catholic Church and the independent sector (which is made up of other religious denominational schools, such as Anglican, Lutheran and Baptist, as well as non-denominational schools). An independent school is a not-for-profit business. The schools participating in the study had an annual recurrent turnover of between $25 and $35 million. The role of a head at an independent school is not dissimilar to that of a CEO of a mid-to-large corporation, accountable to their governing body for the day-to-day running of the school including human resource management (both teaching and non-teaching staff), financial management (including payroll, superannuation, funding, loans and fees), asset development, governance management, public relations, crisis management, risk and compliance, philanthropy, student management, and directions in curriculum and pedagogy. Heads in independent schools are primarily responsible for the implementation of the vision and strategic plan set by the governing body. Because the role of a head in an independent school is diverse and complex, it could be argued that the findings of the study would not only be applicable in an educational context, but would translate across other sectors and into the corporate world. The lessons learnt from these highly trusted leaders are applicable to those in the not-for-profit and for-profit worlds.

Two tools were used in Phase One, the Transformational Leadership Measurement (TLM) tool, used extensively in studies on leadership, and the Organisational Trust Inventory (OTI). It is interesting, that while there isn't an agreed definition for trust, you can measure it. In 1997 two academics, Nyhan and Marlow, developed a tool with 12 questions, four that measure trust in leadership and eight that measure trust in the organisation. Since its development the tool has been used in many studies, proving to be a very reliable measure of leadership and organisational trust.

Large schools across Australia and New Zealand (large being defined as a staff greater than 140) were invited to be part of Phase One. Trust is easier to develop in smaller institutions because you have more opportunity to interact with individuals and develop relationships; it is much harder to build when you are responsible for a lot of people. The study was not about a person's character or personality, but about their leadership practices. In total, 28 schools participated in Phase One with 1252 people completing the two surveys (TLM and OTI) about their leader. Of these, 19 schools returned statistically reliable data; that is, a high enough percentage of the staff completed the surveys to say that the data was 95 per cent accurate with an acceptable margin (+/-) of error. From that data six leaders were identified and approached to be part of Phase Two of the research. In the end, only four leaders were studied because I had reached what is known as 'data saturation': no new data was being revealed and so the additional two cases were not required.

Several interesting things were revealed from the data in Phase One. Firstly, it showed that all leaders who participated in the initial phase were trusted to a degree leading me to conclude that it isn't a question as to whether or not you are trustworthy, but rather, how much you are trusted. We often think that trust is something you grow. My study showed that this wasn't the case. Of the leaders chosen for the second phase of the research, one had been at their current organisation for one year, another 16 years. The person who returned the lowest level of trust had been at their organisation for 17 years. The data also showed that the person's character or personality had nothing to do with the level of trust they enjoyed. Two of the leaders chosen for the final phase were introverts, two were extroverts; two were female and two were male. From the data I could say with confidence that trust had nothing to do with tenure or personality, and everything to do with how the leaders led.

Finally, the data showed a strong correlation (r=0.92) between trust and transformational leadership; meaning, a leader was less likely to be able to achieve a strategic vision without a high level of trust.

Phase Two of the study involved me visiting the leaders at their schools. I spent a week in each, shadowing them to observe their behaviours and conducting interviews. I invited staff to come and tell me stories as to why they trusted their head. I wasn't interested in words like *integrity* or *honesty*, I was interested in what leaders did and how that action made people feel. While these people didn't know me, they came and told me of the time that their head did something that engendered trust. I listened until I reached data saturation.

In all, across all four schools, I interviewed 106 staff members. This stage of the research also involved an extensive interview with the head and the Chair of the governing body. I then triangulated the data by sending out a survey to the staff of each of the four schools. That survey was created using the data collected in the interviews for each individual school. From those surveys I was able to ascertain how many staff valued a particular practice and how prominent it was in their leader's behaviour. The surveys enabled me to refine the specific practices that each leader was exhibiting. I then looked for them in action as I shadowed each head and sat in on meetings they held. Each leader used between 11 and 15 practices, but more practices didn't translate into a higher level of trust, in fact, the most trusted leader only employed 12 practices. In all, between all four leaders, 21 practices were identified.

The final stage of the research was to carry out a cross-case analysis. The purpose of this exercise was to compare and contrast each leader's context, their personalities and their leadership practice. That work revealed 10 leadership practices common between all four leaders, practices that were engendering high levels of trust of their staff and enabling them to achieve the vision they had for their school.

Following the PhD (which was nominated for an outstanding thesis award and won an Executive Dean's Commendation) I used the findings to develop a tool to measure a leader's effectiveness in each of those 10 practices. I tested the tool with leaders across the country and found it to be a very reliable measure, not only of trust but also of transformational leadership. Since then, the tool has been used as an appraisal (or performance) measure by leaders across the globe, helping them to grow their practice.

SOURCES

BOOKS AND JOURNAL ARTICLES

Barsade, S and O'Neill, O 2014, 'What's love got to do with it? A longitudinal study of the culture of companionate love and client outcomes in a long-term care setting', *Administrative Science Quarterly*, Sage Journals, vol. 59, no. 4, pp. 551–98.

Bass B, 1985, *Leadership and Performance Beyond Expectations*, Free Press, New York.

Beltran-Aroca C, Girela-Lopez E, Collazo-Chao E, Montero-Pérez-Barquero M, Muñoz-Villanueva MC 2016, 'Confidentiality breaches in clinical practice: What happens in hospitals?', *BMC Medical Ethics*, vol. 17 no. 52 <https://bmcmedethics.biomedcentral.com/articles/10.1186/s12910-016-0136-y>

Bhatia, R 2019, 'Data breach exposes confidential information at IT company HCL', *Information Security Newspaper*, Viewed on 19 September 2019 <https://www.securitynewspaper.com/2019/05/21/data-breach-exposes-confidential-information-at-it-company-hcl/>.

Brooks, D 2015, *The Road to Character*, Penguin, New York.

Burns JM, 2009, *Leadership*, Harper Collins, New York.

Collins, J 2001, *Good to Great*, Century, London.

Commonwealth Scientific and Industrial Research Organisation (CSIRO) 2019, *Australian National Outlook 2019*, CSIRO.

Covey, S and Merrill, R 2008, *The Speed of Trust: The one thing that changes everything*, Free press, New York.

De Crespigny, R 2018, *Fly!: Life lessons from the cockpit of QF32*, Viking, Melbourne.

Doffman, Z 2019, 'Facebook has just been caught spying on users' private messages and data – again', *Forbes*, viewed 19 September 2019, <https://www.forbes.com/sites/zakdoffman/2019/01/30/facebook-has-just-been-caught-spying-on-users-private-messages-and-data-again/#57887a8d31ce>.

Dweck, C 2012, *Mindset: Changing the way you think to fulfil your potential*, Constable and Robinson, London.

Eger, E 2018, *The Choice: Even in hell hope can flower*, Penguin, London.

Everett, L 2017, 'CEO Visibility – a new dimension of branding', *The CEO Magazine*, viewed 19 September 2019, <http://media.the-ceo-magazine.com/guest/ceo-visibility-new-dimension-branding>.

Gerstacker, D 2014, 'Sitting is the new smoking: 7 ways a sedentary lifestyle is killing you', *The Active Times*, viewed 22 July 2019, <https://www.theactivetimes.com/sitting-new-smoking-7-ways-sedentary-lifestyle-killing-you>.

Giacoman, A 2017, 'The Caring Leader', *strategy+business*, viewed 19 September 2019, <https://www.strategy-business.com/blog/The-Caring-Leader?gko=71c53>.

Goulston, M 2013, 'How to Give a Meaningful "Thank You"', Harvard Business Review, viewed 13 November 2019, < https://hbr.org/2013/02/how-to-give-a-meaningful-thank>.

Hall, V 2009, *The Truth About Trust in Business: How to enrich the bottom line, improve retention, and build valuable relationships for success*, Emerald Book Company, Austin.

Higginbottom, K 2018, 'The Perils of an Absentee Boss', *Forbes Magazine*, viewed 5 October 2018, <https://www.forbes.com/sites/karenhigginbottom/2018/10/05/the-perils-of-an-absentee-boss/#23e26bd34293>.

Hurley, R 2006, 'The Decision to Trust', *Harvard Business Review*, viewed 13 November 2019, < https://hbr.org/2006/09/the-decision-to-trust>.

Kaplan J, 2015, *The Gratitude Diaries,* Dutton, New York.

Kouzes, J and Posner, B 2003, *Credibility: How leaders gain and lose it, why people demand it,* Jossey-Bass, San Francisco.

Mackay, H 2013, *The Good Life: What makes a life worth living?*, Pan Macmillan Australia, Sydney.

McCraty, R, Barrios-Chopli, B, Rozmann, D, Atkinson, M and Watkins, A 1998, 'The impact of a new emotional self-management program on stress, emotions, heart rate variability, DHEA and cortisol', *Integrative Physiological and Behavioral Science*, vol. 33, no. 2, pp. 151–60, <https://link.springer.com/article/10.1007%2FBF02688660>.

McCullough, M, Emmons, R and Tsang, J-A 2002, 'The Grateful Disposition: A conceptual and empirical topography', in *Journal of Personality and Social Psychology*, vol. 82, no. 1, pp. 112–27, <http://psycnet.apa.org/fulltext/2001-05824-010.html>.

Peck, S 1978, *The Road Less Travelled: A new psychology of love, traditional values and spiritual growth,* Touchstone, New York.

Pink, D 2009, *Drive: The surprising truth about what motivates us*, Riverhead Books, New York.

Reina, D and Reina, M 2006, *Trust and Betrayal in the Workplace: Building effective relationships in your organisation*, 2nd edn, Berrett-Koehler, San Francisco.

Rogers, C 1961, *On Becoming a Person: A therapist's view of psychotherapy*, Houghton Mifflin Harcourt, London.

Sales, L 2018, *An Ordinary Day: Blindsides, resilience and what happens after the worst day of your life*, Hamish Hamilton, Melbourne.

Sergiovanni, T 2005, *Strengthening the Heartbeat: Leading and learning together in schools*, 1st edn, Jossey-Bass, San Francisco.

Sheridan, G 2018, *God is Good For You: A defence of Christianity in troubled times*, Allen and Unwin, Sydney.

Silverstein, S 1964, *The Giving Tree*, 1st edn, Harper Collins, New York.

Solomon, L 2015, 'The Top Complaints from Employees about their Leaders', *Harvard Business Review*, viewed 19 September 2019, <https://hbr.org/2015/06/the-top-complaints-from-employees-about-their-leaders>.

Stevens, M 2016, 'Aurizon's Lance Hockridge changes trains for good', *Financial Review*, viewed 19 September 2019, < https://www.afr.com/business/infrastructure/aurizons-lance-hockridge-changes-trains-for-good-20161130-gt0yjh>.

Watson, C 2018, 'The key moment from Mark Zuckerberg's testimony to Congress', *The Guardian*, viewed 19 September 2019, <https://www.theguardian.com/technology/2018/apr/11/mark-zuckerbergs-testimony-to-congress-the-key-moments>.

White, P and Chapman G, 2019, *The 5 Languages of Appreciation in the Workplace,* Northfield Publishing, Chicago.

White, P 2014, '6 reasons why your boss doesn't thank you enough (or ever)', *The Business Journals*, viewed 19 September 2019, <https://www.bizjournals.com/bizjournals/how-to/growth-strategies/2014/12/6-reasons-why-your-boss-doesnt-thank-you-enough-or.html>.

Wolff, S 1998, 'The Role of Caring Behavior and Peer Feedback in Creating Team Effectiveness', Dissertation, Boston University Graduate School of Management, Boston.

Zak, P 2017, *Trust Factor: The science of creating high-performance companies*, 1st edn, Amacom, Nashville.